CONVERSATIONS WITH JOSEPH FLUMMERFELT

Thoughts on Conducting, Music, and Musicians

DONALD NALLY

THE SCARECROW PRESS, INC.
Lanham • Toronto • Plymouth, UK
2010

Published by Scarecrow Press, Inc.
A wholly owned subsidiary of The Rowman & Littlefield Publishing Group, Inc.
4501 Forbes Boulevard, Suite 200, Lanham, Maryland 20706
http://www.scarecrowpress.com

Estover Road, Plymouth PL6 7PY, United Kingdom

British Library Cataloguing in Publication Information Available

Library of Congress Cataloging-in-Publication Data

Flummerfelt, Joseph.
   Conversations with Joseph Flummerfelt : thoughts on conducting, music, and
musicians / Donald Nally.
      p. cm.
   Includes bibliographical references and index.
   Discography: (p.   ).
   ISBN 978-0-8108-6976-9 (pbk. : alk. paper)
   1. Flummerfelt, Joseph—Interviews. 2. Conductors (Music)—United States—
Interviews. 3. Choral conducting. I. Nally, Donald, 1960–. II. Title.
ML422.F64A5 2010
782.5092—dc22   2010000420

Printed in the United States of America

for Joe

[handwritten inscription: "To [name] with best wishes with warm [wishes]" and signature dated "May 1st 2012"]

Alone with his longing, he lies down on his bed
and sings a lament; everything seems too large,
the steadings and the fields.

—*Beowulf*, 2460–63, trans. by Seamus Heaney

CONTENTS

FOREWORD
Kurt Masur

I have been quoted many times as saying that I made the New York Philharmonic more democratic. What I mean by this is that we have created a situation of great trust in a musical environment—great freedom through discipline. It took quite some time for the musicians to feel free to speak to me directly about artistic matters (even differences), and for me to speak openly to them. In time, we found our way to a collaboration that was direct and open; simply put, we shared the same goals and knew this of each other. The rest was inevitable.

In the beginning of my time in New York, I knew only one person directly involved with the Philharmonic. This was Joe Flummerfelt, with whose great choir from Westminster Choir College I had already collaborated on New York performances of Brahms's *Requiem* with its premiering orchestra, Leipzig Gewandhaus. Meeting Joe's choir was like meeting someone I had known for many years; it was as if, without having ever previously met, we had already done all the work of trust and openness by the perfect alignment of what we feel music is. The depth of understanding, the attention to detail (always related to the meaning of the text), the emotional quality of the colors—these are all things I would have asked of him but never had to. Then we moved to New York and took up a collaboration of joy with the Philharmonic and Joe's choirs. I was told that New York audiences don't like choral pieces, but I ignored this; I knew we could offer them something very special through the combination of this great orchestra and Joe's wonderful choirs. And we did. We forged forward with the works of Johann Sebastian Bach and achieved wonderfully stylistic performances with contemporary players and singers. In fact, the Bach performances are among the greatest achievements of the orchestra in my time, because everyone understood the spirit of these performances; everyone committed. And it is safe to say that of all the many concerts I conducted with the Philharmonic, I liked the choral performances most of all.

The pinnacle of these experiences was the Brahms performance following 9/11. That performance was, of course, unforgettable. Brahms's masterpiece doesn't give us the opportunity for sadness; instead, it describes how to overcome the fear to die, it describes the beauty of life, and it gives us hope. We are absolutely clear that this Requiem never has to be sentimental, never is really full of sadness; it is full of love. It was the only piece we could have done at that time, and I already knew from experience of Joe's profound relationship with that work. In the end, it was the most touching experience of any concert in my life; everyone who sang or played in that performance felt that we had the opportunity to heal wounds. Never again will I achieve that uniqueness, when an audience is so united, when they are ready to go away no longer fearing to die. And this success was largely due to the unspoken understanding between conductor and chorus master, who share a profound love of such works as well as a love for the audience, for the musicians with whom they work, and for each other. Love is fundamental to Joe, to the sound he invites from his choirs, and to the music they produce.

And so it is with love, and great rejoicing, that we welcome this book of Joe's ideas and philosophies. In a world that moves so quickly, that often skims over those issues fundamental to art—meaning, depth, and truth—it is vital that a voice like Joe Flummerfelt's be heard for generations to come, to inspire and inform musicians of all kinds toward rehearsals and performances of substance. Yes, the technical aspects of music-making are necessary and never lacking with Joe's choirs, but it is the connection to the body—to the breath, and to the soul—and the trust and openness with which this is achieved that has made me a lifelong friend and devotee of Joe's conducting. Sharing these ideas, as he did readily with all those he touched in New York, will open up and expand worlds to many who have not had the good fortune to work with this extraordinary musician and to know this great man.

PREFACE

I've probably spent a collective year of long evenings sitting in one bar or another in Spoleto, Italy. On one of those nights, I had a consuming conversation with Joe Flummerfelt in which he told me he would like to someday write a book entitled *The Crossing*—named for that perfect alignment of cognitive and intuitive that allows art to happen: the meeting of the X and Y, yin and yang, vertical and horizontal. The conversation stuck with me; *the crossing*, as an idea, touched something in my own need to communicate—to "get across," to reach. Eventually, my cofounder, Jeff Dinsmore, and I would name an ensemble for it. The idea, now a name, seemed to capture so many aspects of who we were and what we wanted to be. And by then we had Cormac McCarthy's novel of the same name as a foundation, with the words "Nor does God whisper through the trees. His voice is not to be mistaken. When men hear it they fall to their knees and their souls are riven and they cry out to Him and there is no fear but only wildness of heart that springs from such longing . . ."

I first met Joe when I auditioned at Westminster Choir College in the spring of 1985. It was a disastrous audition; my flight from Chicago, where I was teaching at the performing arts high school and largely concerned with show tunes and music history, was hours late and wrought with the tension of thunderstorms while in the air. I arrived at my parents' home in Bucks County at about two in the morning, was back up at six to drive to Princeton for a nine o'clock theory entrance exam, followed by voice and conducting auditions, the latter with the Westminster Choir. I was precocious, determined, and a mess. For my voice audition I chose a song of Anton Webern, thinking it nicely balanced the audition repertoire of Poulenc's *Timor et tremor* and Fauré's *Cantique de Jean Racine*. (I was wrong.) Exhausted, I choked on the Webern, barely could demonstrate even a rudimentary sight-singing ability, and was cranky in the choral "finale" of the day, turning to the accompanist at one point to bark, "Don't drag." (It turns out that this player, Glenn Parker, one of the most musically and intellectually gifted people I've known, later became my best friend—after some work. He *never* dragged.) Somehow in this chaos, however, Joseph Flummerfelt saw something in me worth an investment, though even he has admitted that he knew he was taking a chance. So I left Chicago for Princeton, not knowing that, through years of observing him and studying with and singing under him, Joe would become the most influential person in my artistic life—inviting such a massive change in how I think about art and of myself as an artist that I can only scarcely recall who I was prior to my work with him. Ignorantly and innocently, I came to sing at Westminster under the greats. I would work harder than I knew I could, face seasons of personal failures and epiphanies, and come to think of my life as an enormous adventure of discovery that, on a particularly beautiful, cool, July evening in 1988, would find me in a bar in Umbria, chatting about art with my teacher and friend.

Nearly ten years after that conversation in Spoleto, at a particularly low time in my life, it occurred to me that Joe, possessed of that humility and self-doubt that lives in all great artists, was never going to write that book himself—and that, maybe, I could contribute something to our art by capturing in words what it is that makes his music-making so unique. So, I sat down with him to listen: to talk about *the crossing*—the idea—to ask him about his life and artistic evolution, and to write that book.

Another ten years have passed since those initial conversations in front of Joe's fireplace in Lawrenceville, New Jersey. We've had many more conversations since. The proposed title has long ago been absorbed into a larger project, as Joe's voice has resonated deeper and more broadly on paper. Much has changed in that time: while remaining at the New York Philharmonic and Spoleto USA, Joe has retired from Westminster Choir College and found a new life as a celebrated guest conductor; I have journeyed in and out of fascinating jobs in several countries; we've seen those towers fall out of the sky on a sun-drenched September day in New York; our country has elected an African-American president. A few of those mentioned in the book have passed on in the time it has taken for the project to mature—for it to take shape as a record of an idea (an artistic personality, a style) that is difficult to chronicle, challenging to elucidate, and eludes tangibility.

In a recent interview for WFMT-Chicago, I made a comparison between the music of David Lang (who won the 2008 Pulitzer Prize in music) and Johannes Brahms—not in compositional style, obviously, since the latter would surely have been perplexed at the former's minimalism. Rather, I was speaking about music that is courageous—music that is so open and direct, so human, you wonder how its composer walks down the street in daylight, knowing what we know of him. Sometimes this kind of music—raw, base, extraordinarily beautiful, intimate—is like lying in bed with your favorite and listening to them softly talk about their feelings, or, perhaps, it's like those moments when, walking alone, you find yourself speaking your thoughts aloud. This is what it is like to know Joe's art. To be a part of it—to sing with that risk—can be at first scary, then exciting and motivating, and finally, when you realize where you've gone—where you are—like the muted voice of my mother, pulling up to the house after a late-night car ride: "Don, we're home." This is why I asked Joe to write this book—not about "comfort," but about "home"—true home, in us, as Brahms found in "An die Heimat": "Gib mir den Frieden zurück, Den ich im Weiten verloren . . ." (Give me back the peace that I have lost in the distance . . .).

　　Isn't that the goal? That we, as conductors, as singers and instrumentalists, as artists or listeners or art lovers, allow music to take us where it will, if we let it? If we, in Joe's words, "get out of the way"? For many of us, conducting is (for better or worse) largely personality—an endless struggle to be a leader of people while keeping our ego out of the music, of inspiring excellence while allowing personal expression, of balancing strength with vulnerability. I set out to make this book with Joe because the vocabulary of his art is not "struggle, ego, and allow." His vocabulary is "invite, listen, and breathe." For some, this will give insight into what a conductor does. For others, it will remind them of things they know—perhaps, instinctively—but lose in the daily routine of music-making, largely administrative, disproportionately weighted toward preparation. For others, this may be a new way of looking at art. For me, it is how it began, sitting in front of a fireplace, listening to my mentor talk about art, ever grateful to be the recorder of these words.

ACKNOWLEDGMENTS

Many artists have contributed to this book in its final incarnation. Among those who helped transcribe, research, edit, and revise are Heather Buchanan, Stephen Costello, Jennifer Gabriel, Steven Gearhart, Ray Killian, Douglas Millar, Albert Pinnsoneault, and Isaac Selya. Special thanks to Elizabeth Braden for her care in meticulously transcribing every word of our hours of conversations and to Marjory Klein and Maren Montalbano Brehm for their invaluable help keeping us organized. Generously offering photographs and memorabilia were William Struhs (Spoleto USA, Charleston), and, at Westminster Choir College of Rider University, Nancy Wicklund (Talbott Library), Anne Sears (External Affairs), and the Alumni Office. Our warm thanks to Maestro Kurt Masur and his assistant Stefana Zorzor Atlas for their great contribution. Finally, and most of all, thank you to the singers who have inspired, challenged, and breathed with us.

INTRODUCTION

Initially, I hoped this book would give the reader the feeling that he or she was sitting in Joseph Flummerfelt's living room listening to us chat, as the conversation naturally meandered from one area of Joe's life to another and back. However, when the tapes from our twelve hours of conversations were transcribed, and after the nine hours of "ums," "of courses," and "all by way of sayings" were edited out, we had more "meandering" than "natural"—a rather random conversation between two enthusiastic but easily distracted musicians. It was a good study in how conversation actually works, but not a good read. One moment we were discussing Igor Stravinsky's ideas on ontological and psychological time and the next we were talking about a chance meeting with Greta Garbo (true, although subsequently victim to an edit for "taste"). So, I set to arranging the conversations into sensible topics that are easier to navigate, and then we filled in the gaps. It turns out that much of the really valuable information lay in the gaps—much of the detail was hidden in the questions the conversation itself provoked.

While our book is meant to be read as an evolving story—and, certainly, as we move further into the book, we gain a deeper understanding of Joe's being—it can also be read, and returned to, by topic. A conductor may want to come back to the chapter "The Crossing," exploring how Joe's ideas on art translate into producing sound. A music lover may want to concentrate at some point on the chapters about Robert Shaw or Leonard Bernstein, while a working musician will find that these autobiographical chapters also contain some of Joe's most insightful observations on making music. A student may want to focus on Joe's descriptions of his teachers and influences and what he gained from each.

Is this a handbook for conductors? A biography? Memoir? Textbook? We feel it is all and none of these. We didn't set out to write an instruction manual; it doesn't tell us how to *do* anything. Instead, it describes how a number of great musicians do it—how they approach their work, how they collaborate, what they're thinking and feeling. It invites us into their insights and confirms Joe's notion that the greatest part of learning happens through assimilation. Simply described, it is a conversation between two choral conductors—Donald, the student, asking questions; Joe, the mentor, answering, while discovering the words that describe his own life and work. When posing questions I imagined myself alternately as a singer, radio interviewer, student of conducting, devoted audience member, peer, orchestral musician, or composer. My questions resulted in a rather strong interviewer presence, which I subsequently diminished so we may hear Joe's voice clearly as he develops each topic from a seed into a multidimensional idea, setting down those views, techniques, and experiences that have led nearly two generations of conductors into strong and influential positions of responsibility in our art.

And, that art? That art is not just choral, nor just conducting. It's not just vocal, nor is it just scholarly. It's not just about preparation, nor is it just about execution. It's definitely not about administering. It's a fully formed, comprehensive art that is physical, cognitive, and spiritual, embodying universal themes. We aspire to attain that in any art and Joe provides a window into how he got there. This is why a description of Robert Shaw's approach to rhythm in Baroque music is also a discussion of the indivisible relationship between text and music *and* a dialogue on conducting technique *and* a conversation about the ability of music to convey emotion. Clearly, within each artist, these issues are difficult, if not impossible, to separate. We all have paradoxical personalities; the bigger the personality, the more pronounced the paradox. In this book, we encounter a world of large personalities.

I find conducting to be a curiously rejuvenating force. How many times have I seen conductors drag themselves silent and exhausted to the pit, only to emerge at the end of an opera to leap onstage for a bow, chatting to anyone and everyone, ready for a night on the town? Music accommodates as many diverse styles and personalities as there are ensembles to be conducted. Music seems to reveal our strengths, while it tolerates our inadequacies. It survives; it seems to know it will outlast us. It is not the intention of our conversation to instruct the reader to act as described here—or even to think similar thoughts or emulate similar gestures. This is simply how one musician, Joe Flummerfelt, the true voice of this book, approaches art; I hope this sparks a moment of recognition in all readers. It's a good read about a fascinating life, and a lot shorter than listening to us talk to each other for twelve hours.

I

THE EARLY YEARS

1

EARLY INFLUENCES

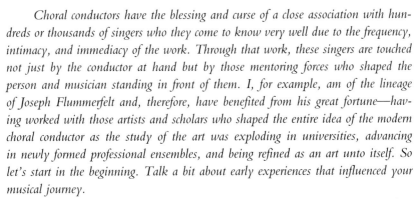

Choral conductors have the blessing and curse of a close association with hundreds or thousands of singers who they come to know very well due to the frequency, intimacy, and immediacy of the work. Through that work, these singers are touched not just by the conductor at hand but by those mentoring forces who shaped the person and musician standing in front of them. I, for example, am of the lineage of Joseph Flummerfelt and, therefore, have benefited from his great fortune—having worked with those artists and scholars who shaped the entire idea of the modern choral conductor as the study of the art was exploding in universities, advancing in newly formed professional ensembles, and being refined as an art unto itself. So let's start in the beginning. Talk a bit about early experiences that influenced your musical journey.

I grew up in Vincennes, Indiana, a town of around twenty thousand in the southern part of the state. My mother was a piano teacher and, in fact, continued to teach until she was ninety-four. I began taking lessons with her when I was about four years old. Before that, I would stand at the piano as she taught me songs. So music was always in my home.

When I was very young, Mother was organist at the First Baptist Church and I would go sit by the organ during choir rehearsals and sometimes when she went to practice. One Sunday, I think I was about five years old, I came home from church, went to the piano, and played the hymn "Stand Up for Jesus," which I had heard in church that morning. Mother rushed in, asking how I had learned that. I answered that I had heard it that morning. So I began to play by ear, and also to improvise.

Throughout my growing-up years, I spent long hours improvising at the piano. This helped a lot when I started playing the organ in church my sophomore year in high school. I had no repertoire at all but was able to improvise preludes and postludes, which really helped fill the gaps. The thing I loved most was playing the hymns. I loved leading the congregational singing from the keyboard. I was unaware of it at the time, but understood some years later, that this was the first sign of my love for getting people to sing. My ability to improvise, for sure, also contributed to my later belief that every performance must have a spontaneous quality that is, in some sense, improvisatory.

My home church, the Disciples of Christ, had a Sunday-evening youth group called Christian Endeavor. I remember playing for the singing from a little blue hymnal filled with gospel oldies like "What a Friend We Have in Jesus," "Blessed Assurance," "Onward Christian Soldiers," and "In the Garden"—hymns I had also played in the morning services. Even though I no longer subscribe to any institutional approach to worship, and certainly not to the theological implications of those hymns, their simple but human sentiment still brings tears to my eyes. I think my need for song to come from some elemental human place started there.

This brings to mind the funeral service of my grandmother. It was in Elnora, Indiana—a simple little country town where my father's parents lived. I think I was around seven or eight when she died. During the service, a gospel quartet sang that well-worn gospel song "It Is Well with My Soul." I remember thinking, even then, that they didn't sound all that good. It was sort of out of tune and the voices didn't fit very well. But hearing it brought a flood of tears. As I later thought about that experience, I understood that those tears had far more to do with the honesty, the directness, the heartfelt outpouring of those simple folks than with the sense of loss of my grandmother. Even though my musical world is long removed from that simple country gospel quartet, their honesty, their unfettered outpouring of something authentic, something deeply human, has continued to influence what I listen for in music.

As for conducting, when I was around twelve my family bought their first record player. With it came a free recording of Handel's *Messiah*, by the Huddersfield Choral Society of England, with Sir Malcolm Sargent[1] conducting. I remember spending hours in front of our living room mirror conducting that recording. Having seen only our local church choir and high school band directors at work (remember, this was before television), I didn't really know what I was doing; yet, responding to the music with some sort of gesture seemed to come naturally. I continued to play organ for church through my high school years, and my only active conducting experience, so to speak, was as drum major of our high school marching band.

In 1954 I went to DePauw University[2] as an organ and church music major. DePauw offered me many opportunities to try my wings as a conductor. It began my freshman year when I conducted a student-written musical. In my junior year I was asked to take over the student-directed opera workshop. Interestingly enough, the first thing I conducted that year was Menotti's[3] *The Medium.* That year I also became director of a talented small group of singers called The Collegians, an ensemble that performed all or part of various Broadway musicals. Additionally, for four years I accompanied the University Choir, which certainly influenced the evolution of my choral journey, since the choirs in the churches I had played for had been pretty ordinary, and my high school had no choral program at all.

After DePauw, you worked at Purdue. Then came Elaine Brown;[4] you spent two years with her in Philadelphia—two influential years.

Yes, I studied with her, both as an intern in Singing City Choir, and at the same time as a graduate student at the old Philadelphia Conservatory of Music.

Certainly, the seeds of my understanding of the binding force of people singing together were planted there. She profoundly understood the quality of community that happens when people converge at the nexus of the composer's impulse. Also, she confronted me in ways that began to force me to get out of my own way.

Also inspiring were her powerful rhythmic drive and her absolute insistence that every singer stay fully connected with, and committed to, every instant of music-making. Yet as time went on, I became concerned that her penchant for constantly making the music exciting rarely allowed it to simply hover. This caused me to begin to think about qualities of movement in music, and that sometimes the line's progress is more horizontal and sometimes it is more vertical. I began to understand that, as conductors, we need to intuitively understand when the line needs a spark of energy, and when it needs to be allowed to proceed on its own terms. Erich Leinsdorf[5] once said, "The art of conducting is knowing when not to conduct." This also brings to mind a quote of Herbert von Karajan's[6] that I recently read, "The art of conducting consists in knowing when to stop conducting, to let the orchestra play." I always tell my students that, while the conductor generates flow, ebb can only be allowed to happen. Thus, in my own conducting, I have tried to manifest the principle that any musical line requires a very subtle interaction of energizing and allowing.

It was a growing experience to be in the midst of the social outreach of Singing City. And, it was certainly important for me to be living next door to a really poor neighborhood in Philadelphia. Because, talk about being a provincial creature—I was! Philadelphia was a real culture shock for me. I came from a very sequestered, Indiana upbringing. Even at DePauw, where I received a wonderful education, it was in the fifties, and we were pretty insulated from the world outside our bucolic campus. So, just being in Philadelphia expanded my world view in so many ways.

Elaine Brown was a great humanitarian who understood, and practiced at the deepest level, how people singing and making music together can be a powerful force to unite those of all races and creeds and create community in the fullest sense of that word. She was fearless in that pursuit, and in the fifties took her fully integrated Singing City choir into the South, which at that time took a lot of courage. Some time later, when the choir was going to sing in Israel, she also insisted that they sing in Jordan—this at a time when no Arab country had any relationship with Israel. I have to say that my years in Philadelphia were not always that comfortable, but being a part of that whole experience was life-changing for me. Many years later I returned to Singing City as their music director, conducting them for five seasons.

Did you study conducting with Elaine?

No, not as such. We talked about a lot of things—life. There is a book called *Zen and the Art of Archery* that Elaine loved. The book speaks of the unity, the interconnectedness, the oneness of the archer and his or her bow. This was a wonderful metaphor for the relationship of conductor to ensemble.[7] In a very real sense, the two become one. For sure, this important little book planted the seed that grew into my belief that the relationship of the conductor to his or her singers is, or ought to be, a circular one. While the conductor quite properly generates shape and dynamic contour, sets the tempo, etc., music-making that truly communicates, that can have a life-changing impact upon both the performers and the audience, only happens when there is an intimacy of connection between the conductor and the singers that creates a space in which the conductor is constantly being informed in the moment by what the singers are generating. Without this communication, instead of being in the moment—in which unplanned, unexpected, hence magical and wonderful things can happen—the conductor stands outside, controlling what he or she thinks ought to happen. For me such performances, however technically proficient, are stillborn. What results is, I believe, preplanned reproduction rather than spontaneous re-creation.

While in Philadelphia you also studied with Vincent Persichetti.[8]

I studied modern harmony with him. He wrote his well-known book on modern harmony more or less out of that course. With him I began to get some insight into how twentieth-century music is put together. To watch him going through the Berg *Lulu Suite*, just playing it on the piano. He'd say, "Well, it wants to do this, and that wants to do that . . ." as if music takes on its own life. And, it does, of course. That made a big impression on me. It contributed to my notion that great music works its own will in a certain way; it has its own organic inevitability, and our responsibility as performers is to internalize the amazing balance of tension and relaxation that exists in all great Western music. We also studied Béla Bartók's *Music for Strings, Percussion, and Celeste*, and again, he did the same thing with that—playing it and talking through it. He was a brilliant musician. He could read anything and he played very complex scores mostly from memory. He was a good composer, and a fine teacher. I also studied composition with him and he thought I should take my little efforts seriously. And you see how I've listened to that.

Talk more about life in Philadelphia.

In my first year I went to the Philadelphia Orchestra concerts every Friday afternoon. I sat in the first balcony, with the ladies who came to the Barclay Hotel for lunch and who often left in the middle of "it-didn't-matter-whatever-the-last-piece-was" to catch the Paoli local back to the Main Line. Ormandy[9] was the conductor and, while it was wonderful to hear that great orchestra, I found myself not fully engaged by the music because the sound never changed. It was always so lush, so robust. I was sort of beating up on myself because I would sometimes lose interest in what the orchestra was playing. But then one week Max Rudolf[10] came to conduct a Brahms Third Symphony, and suddenly there was color range and an intensity that was very different. I especially remember one moment when he turned to the celli to invite a certain solo passage. The sound that emerged just blew me away. And that was the beginning of the realization of the profound effect a conductor has on the sound of the orchestra.

The first *Messiah* I experienced was a performance Singing City did with Ormandy. I remember him rearing back on his haunches to elicit an overblown, bulbous crescendo in some passage or other. And he said, "Well, Mr. Handel didn't write it, but that's what he would want." Even then I had a sense that Ormandy's approach to the score was too much about him. Yet, still today I can respond to recordings of what we now consider overly Romantic readings of *Messiah* with conductors like Sir Thomas Beecham,[11] who may not have been historically informed by today's standards, but grew out of a deep level of artistry, and were also no doubt influenced by the knowledge that Handel himself used large forces for some of his own performances.

And how many people were in that choir?

Well over a hundred, I think. Another great Philadelphia experience happened because of Singing City. I had my first contact with Leonard Bernstein there, though not a personal one. The Philadelphia Academy of Music used to have special fund-raising galas. The one I'm referring to had a patriotic theme, and Singing City was asked to conclude the evening singing Wilhousky's[12] "Battle Hymn of the Republic." Also on the program were the Poulenc Organ Concerto, some Verdi opera quartet, and the *Overture to Candide*. Bernstein conducted half of it, and William Smith,[13] the orchestra's associate conductor, conducted the other half. I'll never forget that experience. It was the morning after John Kennedy was inaugurated; Bernstein had attended, and had, no doubt, celebrated mightily. All of us in the choir were excitedly awaiting the appearance of the fabled maestro. He walked on stage, clearly a little the worse for wear. I remember he was wearing a red turtleneck and a blue blazer. He opens the score (I'm sure he hadn't looked at it before), got this disdainful look on his face, and said, "OK, let's go." So we started through, and we got to the "In the beauty of the lilies" section, and he stopped and said, "What's this . . . kind of like Fred Waring?"[14] And we said, "Yeah," and he said, "OK," and conducted onward, understanding intuitively how to proceed. Needless to say, the performance was very exciting.

And then—now this is interesting, how things come full circle—I stayed for the orchestra rehearsal; he was rehearsing the *Overture to Candide*. I remember him trying to get the orchestra to loosen up. I was hiding in one of the side boxes—a big proscenium box down front—watching him work. It was so inspiring. Can you imagine what it felt like for a twenty-something kid to hear that fabulous piece rehearsed by that legendary conductor, who just happened to be its composer? How could I have possibly imagined that just about ten years later I was to begin collaborating with this astounding musician in a series of recordings and performances with the Westminster Symphonic Choir and the New York Philharmonic?

Now, the closure to that, for me personally—the bookend, really—came just after he died. One month from the day he died, Carnegie Hall mounted a memorial concert with invited performers and conductors from all over the world; the orchestra was made up of players from all the orchestras he had worked with. The Westminster Symphonic Choir was invited to open the concert with the chorale from his Mass and close with the last movement of the *Chichester Psalms*. I was sitting in the dress rehearsal for the concert, and Christa Ludwig[15] had just finished singing Mahler's "Ich bin der Welt abhanden gekommen." James Levine was conducting. The program indicated that next were to be "works" or "selections" from *Candide*. At that moment, the concertmaster of the Vienna Philharmonic was sitting principal. I'll never forget what happened. All of a sudden he stood up, gave a couple of clicks with his bow, and off they went, playing the *Overture to Candide*. There was no conductor, but Bernstein's spirit was surely on the podium. And sitting there, I remembered the first time I'd seen him conduct an orchestra. It was that very piece. Oh my God. Since that time, the New York Philharmonic always performs that piece without conductor.

Some more influences on your work: Julius Herford.[16]

I encountered Herford when I was twenty-one years old. I learned of him because, in 1958, I asked the director of the music school at DePauw to write Robert Shaw[17] and ask if I could go to Cleveland to watch Shaw rehearse the Cleveland Orchestra Chorus. His assistant wrote back and said I could come (he was doing the B Minor Mass) and see Mr. Shaw afterwards. I can still picture the rehearsal somewhere in Severance Hall. Shaw was on the stage and the choir was seated in a sort of small auditorium. Needless to say, I was very inspired. Afterward, he offered to take me out for a beer. We rode to some bar in his recently acquired Bentley, and he said, "You should see the engine; it looks like an ice cream machine." During our talk I asked him whom I should study with and he said "Julius

Herford." He told me that he was doing a workshop with Herford in San Diego the following summer.[18]

I immediately knew I had to go. So, I went home, called my folks, and told them that for my graduation gift from college, I wanted to go to the San Diego workshop the following summer. As the time approached, I got a notice that Mr. Shaw was alas indisposed, and Roger Wagner[19] was going to be there with Julius Herford. I thought, "Well, I'll go anyway," since I knew Roger Wagner from his recordings. I was initially disappointed that it was Wagner rather than Shaw, but it turned out to be an amazing summer. Wagner was a terrific musician. Here I was, a twenty-one year old kid who hardly knew any choral literature and the repertoire that summer included *Missa solemnis*, *Matthew Passion*, Bach's Cantata no. 4, *Damnation of Faust*—all new to me. The program involved Julius Herford lecturing every morning for about three hours on one of the works, and that afternoon we rehearsed the work he was discussing. Each section culminated in Wagner conducting a performance of that particular work with the San Diego Symphony. Well, you talk about opening up my world! To have Julius Herford talk about Bach and Beethoven, to have him apply his barline analysis to these works,[20] to experience his incredible spirit, and his whole approach to meaning in music. It was just an amazing experience.

Why was Roger Wagner so influential in the States?

Well, he was an enormously gifted man. I remember, once, when I was judging a festival with Gregg Smith[21] and Norman Luboff[22] I asked them during dinner to talk about Roger Wagner. They knew Roger really well because they were all West Coast people, and both Gregg and Norman said that Roger was the most gifted choral conductor of that time. By that time, I had already collaborated with Roger. Before I was hired at Westminster, he had been engaged to take the Westminster Choir on tour during what turned out to be my first year as the director. So my first weeks at Westminster were spent preparing the Westminster Choir for Roger. A year or so later he asked me to prepare the New York Choral Society for a *Missa solemnis*, which he was conducting in Carnegie Hall.

Talk about him as a major choral figure in the United States.

He was enormously musical; he created a wonderful sound. He had a natural, very evocative gestural gift. He was a fine, fine musician; I think he was trained as an organist. He organized the Roger Wagner Chorale, toured widely, and did a lot of recording. What Robert Shaw did on the East Coast, Roger did on the West Coast. They were both about the same age; they both studied with Herford. Roger's strength was works like the Fauré and Duruflé *Requiems*. He grew out of the Gregorian tradition, was raised Roman Catholic. I don't think that Bach and Beethoven were his strong suit, but *Damnation of Faust*, for example, was marvelous because he was born in France and spoke fluent French, and thus had a certain innate understanding of French musical style and how it is bound to the language.

What was it about Herford?

He was always probing beneath the music to understand what motivated it—the human impulse behind it. I suppose it is that as much as anything. Also, his analytical methods, his bar line analysis—which I certainly learned that summer, or at least got an introduction to—and thus a whole way of thinking about music, a new way of organizing it that continues today to influence how I study a score. He was a great musician, a great teacher, and a great human spirit. You know, he was Shaw's principal teacher. And Robert later distanced himself from him. Maybe because Herford had such specific ideas about how a given work should be performed and Robert needed to go his own way. Later Herford went on to influence many students as a professor at the Indiana University School of Music.

Did he conduct?

Yes—it was really not very effective. Because he kept saying, "Softer, and softer," and made everybody so tight, afraid to sing. But he always brought great insight on the music. Subsequently, because he and Elaine had this strong connection, I got to experience him in a number of her workshops. I was even his assistant for a summer or two.

But, that summer, it was like a big window, a big door that was opened—a way of thinking about music, which has had a profound influence on me, because it is at the core of what I believe: how music symbolizes the text and the search for meaning therein.

Then you went to the University of Illinois at Urbana-Champaign to study with Harold Decker.[23] Why did Decker become so important to your generation of conductors?

Well, in the first place, U of I was one of the earliest doctoral choral programs of substance. I ended up going there because, while I was in Philadelphia studying with Elaine Brown in 1962, Harold, who had been on sabbatical in Europe, came through Philadelphia. We met, had a long talk, and I was very impressed with him. Because I was so taken with him personally, and of course, because I knew well the reputation of his program, I decided, without looking further, to go there. And you're right; it's amazing—astounding—to list the folks who are and were in leadership positions in this country who came through that program. It fed on itself, because some good folks went, and then others heard about it because of those good folks, and it kept flowing. Harold wanted me to take over the program when he retired, and I seriously considered doing so, because I had spent two fulfilling years there, and because I dearly loved the school and the program. Harold was a wonderful human being, a man and a musician of great integrity.

In addition to the strength of the choral program, U of I had a very distinguished faculty that included people like musicologist Alex Ringer,[24] pianist Soulima Stravinsky,[25] early-music specialist George Hunter,[26] and so many others. What also made my experience there so special was that Harold turned the Concert Choir over to me in my second year while he went on sabbatical. What a learning experience that was.

Do you remember any of the literature you did?

We did a Palestrina mass, the Stravinsky *Psalms* with two pianos, some Brahms, and a lot more. I remember the Stravinsky caused something of a stir. We performed it with two pianos, and many who were skeptical of the piece working without instruments, especially some of the faculty, thought it worked very well. With the Palestrina Mass, I began to grapple with the issue of getting rid of the bar line and regrouping each melodic line according to its contour, rhythmic construction and, of course, relationship to the text. I went through the score, an old Marks edition, and rebarred the whole piece [see figure 1.1]. I gave these to the graduate student section leaders, and each section learned the piece separately without the choir ever having read through it together. I'll never forget the moment when we first put the four parts together; it was just amazing. One could really hear the independence of each line.

Figure 1.1. Palestrina's "Sicut cervus desiderat," with Flummerfelt's rebarring. Key: | = 3/2, ⌐ ⌐ = 4/4, ^ = 3/4, and ∟ = 2/4 (There is no barring if a 4/4 pattern falls within the printed barline.)

⎯⎯⎯⎯⎯ ∞∞∞ ⎯⎯⎯⎯⎯

So, the influence of Harold?

Certainly, I was introduced to a lot of interesting music, including several world premieres of works written by U of I composers. Also, rarely performed major twentieth-century works like the Bartók *Cantata Profana,* which was quite an undertaking. But, more importantly, he was so generous; the warmth and musicality of his choral work was compelling. There was not an egomaniacal bone in his body, just a complete, warm, and caring human being.

NOTES

1. British conductor Malcolm Sargent, 1895 (Ashford) to 1967 (London), worked regularly with the Royal Choral Society, the London Philharmonic, Liverpool Philharmonic, and the BBC Symphony. He was noted for his interpretations of the music of Elgar, Holst, Britten, and Walton and was chief conductor of the Proms from 1948 to 1967.

2. Joe received an undergraduate degree at DePauw University, a liberal arts college with a school of music in Greencastle, Indiana, in 1958; he returned to serve on the faculty from 1964 to 1968.

3. Italian composer Gian Carlo Menotti, 1911 (Cadigliano) to 2007 (Monte Carlo), studied composition at the Curtis Institute of Music, where he met his partner of many years, Samuel Barber. He achieved great fame in the 1950s for operas produced on Broadway, won two Pulitzer Prizes—for *The Consul* (1950) and *The Saint of Bleecker Street* (1955)—and composed the first opera for television on a commission from NBC, *Amahl and the Night Visitors* (1951). He founded Il Festival dei Due Mondi in Spoleto, Italy in 1958, which expanded to Charleston, South Carolina as Spoleto USA in 1977.

4. Elaine Brown, 1910 (Ridgeway, Pennsylvania) to 1997 (Philadelphia), conducted and taught at Temple University, Westminster Choir College, the Juilliard School, and Union Seminary. She founded Singing City Choir in Philadelphia in 1948, which she conducted nearly forty years.

5. Erich Leinsdorf, 1912 (Vienna) to 1993 (Zürich), was an assistant to Arturo Toscanini and Bruno Walter at Salzburg, then moved to the United States and became a citizen in 1933. He was music director at Cleveland and Boston symphonies, made many recordings with the Los Angeles Philharmonic, and for many years was "head of German literature" at the Metropolitan Opera. His book *The Composer's Advocate: A Radical Orthodoxy for Musicians* (Yale University Press, 1981) is essential reading for young conductors.

6. Herbert von Karajan, 1908 (Salzburg) to 1989 (Anif, near Salzburg), first conducted the Berlin Philharmonic in 1938 and was named Music Director for Life in 1956; he was widely recorded by Deutsche Grammophon.

7. In Elaine Brown's words: "As singers and conductors we need to ask: Does the music we make reflect integrity? Does it relate to life, and where and how it is lived? Does it possess the spontaneity and wonder of a child? Is it so permeated with sober awareness that it affects the musician who cares and relates to life around him so that he can never again be invulnerable, immune, or oblivious?"

8. Vincent Persichetti, 1915 (Philadelphia) to 1987 (Philadelphia), was professor of Composition at Philadelphia Conservatory, the Juilliard School, and the Curtis Institute of Music. A prolific and facile composer, he achieved national fame from the press coverage and success of *A Lincoln Address* (1973). He was Flummerfelt's composition teacher at Philadelphia Conservatory.

9. Eugene Ormandy (born Jenö Blau), 1899 (Budapest) to 1985 (Philadelphia), emigrated to the United States in 1921; he was at first concertmaster of the New York Theatre Orchestra, then music director of the Philadelphia Orchestra (1938–1980). He inherited the famed "Philadelphia sound" from Leopold Stokowski and continued the Romantic tradition in orchestral playing into a time when it was falling out of fashion.

10. Max Rudolf, 1902 (Frankfurt am Main) to 1995 (Philadelphia), emigrated from Germany to the United States in 1940, becoming a citizen in 1945. He was a regular conductor at the Metropolitan Opera and was music director of the Cincinnati Symphony Orchestra. He taught for many years at the Curtis Institute of Music and his book *The Grammar of Conducting: A Comprehensive Guide to Baton Technique and Interpretation* (1950) is widely used in the field.

11. Sir Thomas Beecham, 1879 (St. Helen's, Liverpool) to 1961 (London), was chief conductor at Covent Garden and the Metropolitan Opera and founded both the London Philharmonic Orchestra and the Royal Philharmonic Orchestra.

12. Peter Wilhousky, 1902 (Passaic, New Jersey) to 1978, was conductor and arranger for Toscanini and the NBC Orchestra in the 1940s. A dedicated high school teacher, he also taught at the Juilliard School and made many translations and arrangements of Slavonic works. He composed the English words to "Carol of the Bells" and his is the most-performed arrangement of "Battle Hymn of the Republic": both were made popular through recordings of the Mormon Tabernacle Choir.

13. William Smith, 1925 to 1993 (Philadelphia), studied as a musicologist and pianist at the University of Pennsylvania. He joined the Philadelphia Orchestra as its principal keyboard player in 1952 and soon after was made assistant conductor. From 1976 until his death in 1993 he was associate conductor.

14. Composer and arranger Fred Waring, 1900 (Tyrone, Pennsylvania) to 1984 (State College, Pennsylvania), conducted his Pennsylvanians—named for his home at Delaware Water Gap, as is his popular publishing company, Shawnee Press—from the 1920s; they sang popular music in lush choral/orchestral arrangements for Hollywood, radio, and television.

15. Mezzo-soprano Christa Ludwig, b. 1928 (Berlin), made her professional debut in 1946 as Orlovsky in *Die Fledermaus* in Frankfurt and made her farewell opera performance in 1994 as Klytemnestra in *Elektra* in Vienna. She is the mezzo-soprano on the 1987 Deutsche Grammophon recording of Mahler's Second Symphony with Bernstein, the New York Philharmonic, and the Westminster Symphonic Choir.

16. German musicologist, conductor, and author Julius Herford, 1901 (Anklam) to 1981 (Bloomington, Indiana), taught at Columbia University, the Juilliard School, and Union Theological Seminary, and served on the faculty at Indiana University (1964–1980). His students included Robert Shaw, Roger Wagner, Lukas Foss, and Flummerfelt. With Harold Decker, he edited *Choral Conducting: A Symposium* (Prentice-Hall, 1973).

17. Known as the dean of American choral conductors, Robert Shaw, 1916 (Red Bluff, California) to 1999 (New Haven, Connecticut), greatly raised the status of such conductors, first through his work with The Robert Shaw Chorale (frequently collaborating with Toscanini and the NBC Orchestra on the radio), the Collegiate Chorale, the Cleveland Orchestra Chorus, and, later, as music director of the Atlanta Symphony.

18. Shaw was music director of the San Diego Symphony from 1953 to 1958. He began presenting workshops in 1945 and continued to do so throughout his life, culminating in the annual Robert Shaw Workshop at Carnegie Hall beginning in 1990. In the early 1960s he coordinated the Workshop in Choral Art at San Diego State College; the chorus appeared on the San Diego Symphony's summer season.

19. French-American conductor and educator Roger Wagner, 1914 (Le Puy, France) to 1992 (Dijon, France), settled in Los Angeles in 1937. He founded the Roger Wagner Chorale in 1946 (which toured and recorded extensively), and later founded and served twenty-three years as conductor of the Los Angeles Master Chorale. He was director of choral activities at University of California, Los Angeles.

20. One of many lasting influences is Herford's method of score analysis. Vance George writes, "Herford taught many of us . . . to grapple with musical structure as a source of music's spiritual energy." For a brief explanation of this method, see George's chapter in *The Oxford Companion to Conducting* (Cambridge University Press, 2003); Herford's more detailed account is found in *Choral Conducting: A Symposium*.

21. Conductor and composer Gregg Smith, b. 1931 (Chicago), studied composition with Leonard Stein (a Schoenberg disciple) and Lukas Foss; he has written over four hundred compositions. He formed the Gregg Smith Singers in New York City in 1955; they have recorded a wealth of contemporary works and won several Grammy awards.

22. Norman Luboff, 1917 (Chicago) to 1987 (Bynum, North Carolina), achieved great success in the late 1940s in Hollywood, scoring and conducting for radio, then television and films. The Norman Luboff Choir, which toured annually from 1963 to 1987, recorded over seventy albums.

23. Harold Decker, 1914 (Belleville, Kansas) to 2003 (Wichita), developed the nation's first doctoral program in choral music at Kansas State University, then chaired the choral department at the University of Illinois from 1957 to 1982. He taught many leaders of Flummerfelt's generation of conductors, including Elmer Thomas (University of Cincinnati), Maurice Casey (Ohio State University), Kenneth Jennings, and Anton Armstrong (both of St. Olaf).

24. Alexander Ringer, 1921 (Berlin) to 2002 (Lansing, Michigan), was a longtime member of the musicology department at the University of Illinois. Of Dutch and Polish descent, he wrote numerous books, including *Arnold Schoenberg: das*

Leben im Werk (2002) and *Schoenberg: The Composer as Jew* (1990), as well as the article "Arnold Schoenberg and the Politics of Jewish Survival" (1979).

25. Son of Igor, Soulima Stravinsky, 1910 (Lausanne) to 1994 (Sarasota, Florida), studied piano with Isidore Philipp and theory and composition with Nadia Boulanger. He moved to the United States in 1948 and joined the piano faculty at the University of Illinois in 1950, teaching and writing books on orchestration and the orchestra.

26. American harpsichordist and musicologist George Hunter was an influential figure in the revival of early music practice, launching the Collegium Musicum, one of the nation's first early-music ensembles, at the University of Illinois in 1950.

2

NADIA BOULANGER AND
CULTURAL INFLUENCES

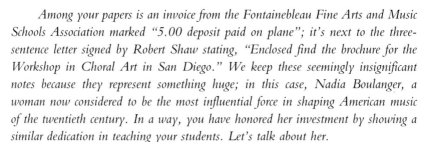

Among your papers is an invoice from the Fontainebleau Fine Arts and Music Schools Association marked "5.00 deposit paid on plane"; it's next to the three-sentence letter signed by Robert Shaw stating, "Enclosed find the brochure for the Workshop in Choral Art in San Diego." We keep these seemingly insignificant notes because they represent something huge; in this case, Nadia Boulanger, a woman now considered to be the most influential force in shaping American music of the twentieth century. In a way, you have honored her investment by showing a similar dedication in teaching your students. Let's talk about her.

Boulanger. A consummate musician. To be in the presence of this woman, who understood so much and knew so much, and was such a life force. A devout Catholic, she possessed a deep spiritual wisdom, coupled with rigorous self-discipline. And, most of all, she was a great artist and a born teacher.

I'll never forget my first day at Fontainebleau, where I had gone to study in the summer of 1964. We had to take a dictation test. Her hands shook at that point; she was seventy-eight, and she was going blind. (As you remember, the last years of her life, she was pretty much totally blind.) So, from memory, she began to play—just the chord progression of the first prelude from *The Well-Tempered Clavier*. We were supposed to take down the root movement, but I could hardly move. I was so transfixed. I mean, the colors and the voice leading . . . oh my God! I had heard her conduct before; I had been to a rehearsal she had done of the Fauré *Requiem* with the New York Philharmonic. Elaine Brown had arranged for me to attend. I'll never forget that rehearsal either. She had come to Philadelphia and given lectures; I heard her give a lecture on Schubert. But remembering that day, how she played that progression of chords so beautifully, still brings tears to my eyes.

Soon after the summer began, she turned the chorus over to me. My responsibility was to prepare the Victoria *O Magnum Mysterium Mass* and Bach's Cantata 58 for a service in the palace chapel at the close of the nine-week summer session. The chorus was "everybody at Fontainebleau"—a "whoever showed up" chorus—which meant architects, artists, and musicians, most of whom were instrumentalists and didn't sing very well. And I was charged with making a chorus out of this. While I was rehearsing she would sit in the middle of the room (talk about intimidating). She always had these young protégés around her and, during one rehearsal, she had one of them sitting at the piano, teaching him to read open score. He was very gifted, as you might expect, but was making a number of mistakes and causing real problems with the rehearsal. Everybody in the room was anxious to see what I was going to do. So, I finally turned around and said, "Mademoiselle, do you suppose we could try it once without the piano?" I was a little terrified, but she understood the situation immediately, and we continued to work a cappella.

How did she teach you conducting?

She didn't teach conducting technique as such. The lessons were mostly about discussing the music. My actual conducting lesson consisted of conducting one of her students at the piano. One day I was conducting the "Benedictus" of Mozart's *Coronation Mass*. It is marked *allegretto*, 2/4. I was trying to be very musical, so I conducted it in 4, making it nearly twice as slow as it should go. She says, "You know, I think it's a little too beautiful." Immediately I understood that my misbegotten attempt to be expressive was completely wrong. If one conducts the "Benedictus" as an *allegretto* in 2, the musical line becomes effortless, and thus in a very profound way symbolizes the effortless, flowing, omnipresent quality of "blessedness." This was such an important lesson for me because I began to understand that often in our attempt to be musical, we end up imposing our ego-driven ideas on the music, and thus we block the composer's voice.

So it's really "music" she taught.

Yes. And rhythmic discipline, through Hindemith's *Elementary Training for Musicians*, which was part of the solfège regimen. As you know,

Donald, that remarkable book is an extensive series of rhythm and sight-singing drills, beginning rather simply and moving to the very complex. Her associate, Mademoiselle Annette Dieudonné[1] taught the course. It was my introduction to the Hindemith book, which contributed enormously to the growth of my own rhythmic skill because we went through most of the book that summer.

What did she hear that other people do not?

First of all, she had such phenomenal ears for all things technical. More importantly, she had a genius for instantly understanding the composer's voice. She was a great human spirit, she was a deeply cultured woman, and she understood so much about people, and about life. I don't think I'll ever encounter anyone else whose life was so totally consumed by music.

I'll never forget one incident that so vividly illustrated the singularity of her musical focus and devotion. She had been away doing something for the Menuhin Festival in Switzerland. (She was very close with the Menuhin[2] family.) So, my lesson had been postponed, and was rescheduled for ten o'clock at night on the day she returned. Here's a woman who is already seventy-eight years old, who had just come from Switzerland that morning, and had taught all day long. She probably had a couple of crusts of bread for lunch; she didn't eat much, at least not at noon. The Fontainebleau palace was closed at night, so you would have to go to a side gate and the guard would let you in. You would then walk across this vast, dark courtyard to the wing where her apartment was and ring the bell. She would then open the window and throw down the key. You would unlock the massive outside door, walk through a dark entryway, and go upstairs. I got to her apartment door, walked in, and couldn't see her. Finally, I saw her hunched over her piano, just playing some sonorities, listening. She had only a couple of minutes, she was probably exhausted, but some musical thing was intriguing her. You talk about devotion—about singular pursuit![3]

So, it was the combination of a phenomenal musical gift, a deeply cultured nature, the rigor with which she approached everything, and the passion to share that with so many students for so many years. Copland went to study with her when he was in his twenties, and she wasn't much older than he was. Yet she was already this looming figure who was to guide the growth of so many major twentieth-century composers.

That was Boulanger. At that point I was off to teach at DePauw the following fall, my first college job. I should probably have delayed it and gone to study with her, but I was too intimidated. Things might have been different, considering her capacity to stretch people. She asked for everything, but she could do it all herself, of course. Her technical mastery was just phenomenal and her ear was flawless. At that rehearsal of the New York Philharmonic, going through a piece by Virgil Thomson[4] (who had also been her student), she stopped and said to the double basses, "Gentlemen, that is not a B-natural, it's a C-flat." Ears beyond belief. It was also in that rehearsal when a remark she made to the violas profoundly impacted my thinking about music-making. It was in the "Libera me" of the Fauré *Requiem*, and the violas were playing a passage of ascending thirds in a big, romantically expressive way. She stopped and said, in her deep voice, with that wonderful French accent, "Gentlemen, you know, sometimes the most expressive thing is to not be expressive at all." Through the years I so often found myself repeating that important idea to my own students. Let the music speak on its own terms; let the composer's voice resonate.

Did you learn about French style from her?

Not as such. We didn't do any French music that summer. But, I do remember a walk in a forest near Fontainebleau and being vividly struck by the attenuation of the trees. I thought, "Isn't it interesting that in things *French* there is this attenuation," and I thought of the Gothic arch. And then I thought of Italy, and the prevalence of plane trees—the look of the Italian landscape—and I thought of Romanesque and its rounded arch. I thought, "Isn't that fascinating? There must be some relationship." So, the idea of things being vertical, and hence more classical, and hence more French, occurred to me in the forest. Whether that was because of Boulanger, I don't know. She didn't talk about things French per se, but the Classical clarity with which she approached musical thought surely influenced me. Also, I was influenced by the many French musical giants who appeared that summer. Robert Casadesus[5] played, and Pierre Bernac[6] did master classes. And, André Marchal[7]—he was a blind organist—played and did master classes. Those men were all her friends.

So I'm sure all that had an impact. But those things that one understands about being French aren't things anyone necessarily teaches you. You're there, you observe, you watch people, how they look, how they react, their gestures, etc. It all relates: the sound of the language, Gothic architecture, and the French fascination with detail and clarity. It's a kind of thing you begin to understand just by being around it.

I asked that because, while I think you are German at heart, you seem to have this clear understanding of French music. It is an entirely different approach—the way you go about making the sound. I am trying to find out where that comes from. Basically, you're just living it.

Yes, but I also think you learn from the music, don't you? I mean, no German composer, however great, could write a chanson. When you think of all the chansons you know—Poulenc, Debussy, Ravel, whatever—the little vignette, the clarity. But then with Brahms there is an inner Sturm und Drang that one doesn't experience in French music. Freud could only have come out of a Germanic culture.

It's fascinating that an affinity for style or period is not necessarily related to our home. You, from Vincennes, Indiana, have this Sturm und Drang that is so innate in your relationship to German music, from Beethoven to Hindemith, even in the ability to prepare Hindemith's Requiem, *and make some sense out of it—a piece I can't make sense out of.*

Well, isn't one's temperament, one's intensity, something one is born with? Also the roots of my own lineage are strongly German. As for the Hindemith, I have trouble with it too. I never really understood Shaw's great devotion to it, other than the fact that he commissioned it.[8] That, and, of course, the whole Lincoln focus and his devotion to Whitman and to the genesis of the poem. During one lesson with Boulanger, I asked her about Hindemith. I don't know how it came up, but I said "I think Hindemith's music began to lose its vitality when he began to compose according to the principles he espoused in his books."[9] And she agreed.

You don't do much Italian music, do you? What have you done?

Well, there were several Italian operas that I prepared for Riccardo Muti[10] and the Philadelphia Orchestra. Verdi: I've programmed the "Ave Maria" many times, and the *Stabat Mater* and *Te Deum* and, of course, both prepared and conducted the *Requiem.* I'm not a great fan of Rossini, but I have prepared the *Stabat Mater* and conducted the *Petite Messe Solenelle.* Vivaldi: I've performed the *Gloria* many times, and the *Magnificat.* As for Puccini, I conducted *La Bohème* once at DePauw and the Westminster Symphonic Choir recorded *Tosca* with Muti and the Philadelphia Orchestra. We also recorded *Pagliacci* with them. For the Spoleto Festival in Italy I prepared the Westminster Choir for a number of Italian operas. But, programming for the Westminster Choir, you're probably right. Actually, I've done those Rossini pieces a couple of times—"La Passeggiata" and the others[11]—and occasional Italian madrigals. I haven't done the Monteverdi Vespers. Of course, I've done Menotti: *The Unicorn, The Medium, Amahl and the Night Visitors,* and recorded his *Missa O Pulchritudo.* Dallapiccola:[12] My first year in Spoleto in 1971 we did the *Canti di Prigionia.* The Italian press loved the performance and he wrote me thanking me for doing it. He never came to Spoleto because he didn't like Gian Carlo. I haven't conducted any Petrassi[13] myself, though, I prepared *Coro di morti* for Muti both with Philadelphia and New York.

NOTES

1. Annette Dieudonné taught solfège to nearly all of Boulanger's students. (Boulanger taught harmony and counterpoint.) Long-time friend of her colleague, she cared for Boulanger in her late years and tended her estate following her death. See Leonard Bernstein's description of his last visit to Boulanger in Bruno Monsaingeon's *Mademoiselle: Conversations with Nadia Boulanger* (Carcanet Press, 1985).

2. The center of this family was American violinist, teacher, and humanitarian Yehudi Menuhin, 1916 (New York City) to 1999 (Berlin); his long career was marked by extraordinary musicianship, the sharing of his gifts, and a dedication to social justice. He was from a distinguished rabbinical dynasty and his two sisters were similarly multitalented artists.

3. It is worth noting a passage from Monsaingeon's *Mademoiselle: Conversations with Nadia Boulanger,* in which Boulanger describes a concert of Menuhin:

> In art we call this inspiration. It is the moment when a man succeeds in grasping his thought, his real thought, right at the core; the moment when we touch the truth, when communion is established. This year there was a concert by Menuhin, an altogether superb concert. He gave a number of encores and the last was the slow movement of Brahms's Sonata in D minor. What happened then was part of an indescribable completeness: the whole house found itself in the grip of the same mute emotion, which created silence of an extraordinary quality. Everyone understood, felt, participated in what he himself must have been feeling. I don't think he will ever forget that moment. In some way it passed beyond him, to a higher level, which we very rarely reach. We are too weak to scale those heights very often, to realise the potential available if we could really commune with ourselves. (37)

4. Virgil Thomson, 1896 (Kansas City, Missouri) to 1989 (New York City), was best known as a music critic in the 1940s, achieving recognition as a composer only

in the second half of his long life. Influenced by Erik Satie and his time in Paris in the 1920s and 1930s, Thomson is known mainly for his operas *Four Saints in Three Acts* (1934) and *The Mother of Us All* (1947).

5. French pianist and composer Robert Casadesus, 1899 (Paris) to 1972 (Paris), preceded Boulanger as director of Fontainebleau, which was founded by his uncle Francis Casadesus. A prodigy, he was among the earliest recording artists. He premiered his Second Piano Concerto with the New York Philharmonic under Stokowski.

6. French baritone Pierre Bernac, 1899 (Paris) to 1979 (Villeneuve-les-Avignon), was a lifelong friend of Poulenc, introducing many of the latter's songs. He was on the faculty at Fontainebleau and wrote two books well known to students of chanson: *The Interpretation of French Song* (1970) and *Francis Poulenc: The Man and His Songs* (1977).

7. French organist and harmonium player André Marchal, 1894 (Paris) to 1980 (Saint-Jean-de-Luz), was born blind. He was a renowned improviser and was instrumental in the twentieth-century French organ revival. He was organist at Saint-Germain-des-Prés, then at Saint-Eustache in Paris.

8. Shaw commissioned Paul Hindemith's *Requiem for Those We Love: When Lilacs Last in the Dooryard Bloom'd,* in 1946. The Whitman poem marks the passing of Abraham Lincoln and his funeral cortege crossing America. It was the passing of Franklin Delano Roosevelt that inspired Shaw to commission the work in memory of that president and all Americans who died in WWII. It is written in a highly contrapuntal style and is full of dense, dark textures.

9. Paul Hindemith's books include *Elementary Training for Musicians* (1945/1946)—the text Joe used with his graduate students; *Traditional Harmony* (two volumes, 1943, 1948); *The Craft of Musical Composition* (1937); and *A Composer's World* (1952).

10. Riccardo Muti, b. 1941 (Naples), became music director of the Maggio Musicale Fiorentino in 1968, securing his international career. From 1979 to 1992 he was music director of the Philadelphia Orchestra, collaborating frequently with the Westminster Choir.

11. "La Passeggiata" is the twelfth and final work of Rossini's *Péchés de vieillesse* (Sins of Old Age), vol. 1, *Album italiano*. There are fourteen volumes of vocal and piano works, written for salon performance, collected in the last decade of Rossini's life and left unpublished.

12. Luigi Dallapiccola, 1904 (Pisino d'Istria—then Austria) to 1975 (Florence), and Luigi Nono were the chief proponents of twelve-tone technique in Italy. Dallapiccola is best known for his operas, especially *Il Prigioniero* (1944–1948). *Canti di Prigionia* is written in a style that could be called a Romantic amalgamation of twelve-tone technique and medieval plainsong.

13. Italian composer Goffredo Petrassi, 1904 (Zagoralo, near Rome) to 2003 (Rome), studied at Accademia Nazionale di Santa Cecilia, Rome. He taught Kenneth Leighton and Peter Maxwell Davies. Drawing on Giacomo Leopardi's (1798–1837) poem *Dialogue between Frederick Ruysch and His Mummies* (which explores death from the viewpoint of the dead), *Coro di morti* (1941) is Petrassi's response to Italy's entrance into World War II.

3

ROBERT SHAW

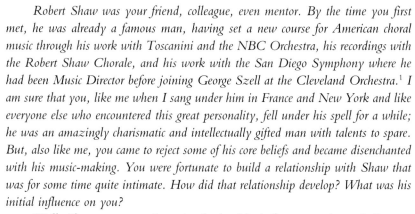

Robert Shaw was your friend, colleague, even mentor. By the time you first met, he was already a famous man, having set a new course for American choral music through his work with Toscanini and the NBC Orchestra, his recordings with the Robert Shaw Chorale, and his work with the San Diego Symphony where he had been Music Director before joining George Szell at the Cleveland Orchestra.[1] I am sure that you, like me when I sang under him in France and New York and like everyone else who encountered this great personality, fell under his spell for a while; he was an amazingly charismatic and intellectually gifted man with talents to spare. But, also like me, you came to reject some of his core beliefs and became disenchanted with his music-making. You were fortunate to build a relationship with Shaw that was for some time quite intimate. How did that relationship develop? What was his initial influence on you?

Well, Shaw at a certain point had a big influence, a huge influence on me.

But you never studied with him. So was it mostly assimilation?

Yes, primarily. I first encountered him when I was a kid—he was on tour with the Shaw Chorale.[2] They performed the Bach *Magnificat* and Honegger's[3] *King David* at the Indiana University auditorium in Bloomington, not too far from my hometown. I'm not sure that it made all that big of an impression, I was so green and so young. Though, something about that performance must have had an impact. Many years later he came to the University of Illinois to do some workshops while I was working on my doctorate. I remember one question I asked him and his response that stuck with me, because it's what ultimately caused me to move away from what had been my complete embrace of everything Robert Shaw did. We were discussing something "after hours." He always was very generous with his time. All the doctoral students would go to his hotel, talk about music, and drink Jack Daniels with him. We were discussing a certain piece, and I asked him about the meaning of the text—the text's relationship to the music. He looked at me and said, "I think that's gobbledygook." I was just devastated. It didn't completely negate my idea, but I was really embarrassed. I never forgot it, and later, at the point when I said, "No, this doesn't make sense to me," I knew it had its beginning there, years before. But his intensity—his rhythmic drive, his cross-beat/cross-bar emphasis, his approach to a line—all that had a huge influence on me until, at a certain point, my musical thinking moved in a different direction.

The really close connection began with Shaw when I joined the faculty of Florida State University as choral director. The summer before, I was working on my dissertation at the University of Illinois. I'll never forget the moment when I got the message from Harold Decker's office that Robert Shaw wanted to talk to me. It was like God had called. I called him back and he said he would like for my choir to perform Ives' *Harvest Home Chorales*, and *Psalm 90*, and Haydn's *Harmonie Mass* with the Atlanta Symphony in November. I gulped and said "Yes."

He was talking about the Florida State Choir . . .

. . . which I had never been in front of! But I had to say yes. Now, in the course of my studies, I'd glanced at the *Harvest Home Chorales* and wondered how in the world anyone conducted those pieces. As you know, Ives has three meters going on simultaneously. Shaw called back a week or so later and asked if I would like to conduct the Ives part of the concert. Because I knew that he had a special relationship with *Psalm 90*, I felt I dared not conduct that, but with a lot of trepidation I agreed to conduct the *Harvest Home Chorales*. To prepare for that, I spent hours at the piano struggling to play some lines and sing another. Gradually that got easier, and I began to feel like I knew the pieces well enough to begin to teach and to conduct them. In Atlanta, during our first run-through with the orchestra, Robert was standing by me on the stage, listening. After we finished, he said, "I've performed these pieces several times, and have recorded them, but what I just heard from your choir was more in tune." Can you imagine what it meant to hear this from that great man? Two years later we did the Penderecki[4] *St. Luke Passion* together. The performance was in the spring of 1971, and Robert came to Tallahassee to spend a week studying the score and talking with me about my solution to the difficulty of realizing some of the aleatoric passages without the addition of some temporal structure. During that week, and the subsequent rehearsals in Atlanta, a deeper bond began to develop between us.

From time to time he would invite me up to Atlanta. I especially remember once when Stokowski was conducting, Robert invited me to come up. By then, Stokowski was a very old man who had to be helped to the podium. Yet, in the concert, with one of the pieces (I think it was *Rite of Spring*), he got such rhythmic drive going in the orchestra that Robert and I, sitting together in the balcony, nearly jumped out of our seats with excitement. We would always go to his house afterwards, drink beer or whatever, and talk about many things. In fact, I first learned about Westminster's interest in me in his living room one of those evenings. He said, "Are you interested in going to Westminster Choir College?" I said, "Tell me more." And he said, "Well, they're trying to find out about you. Their president's trying to get ahold of me. I'll talk to them if you want me to." So, that's how I found out Westminster was interested in me. As I was considering what I knew would be a life-changing decision, Robert invited me to spend a week with him in Aspen where he was conducting *Missa solemnis*. Mostly, just to talk about Westminster. We talked a lot about that, and about much more . . . all by way of saying there was a lot of contact, both personal and musical, for a number of years.

When I arrived at Westminster, they had just launched the Summer Session[5] and they wanted a choral centerpiece. I called Robert and asked if he would come up for the following summer, and that was the beginning of his two-week workshops at Westminster that continued for many summers. In those early summers I was his major gofer, so we spent a lot of time together.

Of course, I went to all of his rehearsals in Bristol Chapel. I still vividly remember the moment when I began to question my embrace of Robert's constant use of cross-beat, cross-bar phrasing. The turning point was a rehearsal of the *St. John Passion*. He was working on the "Lasset uns den nicht" (the "gambling for the garments" chorus) and he had the choir leading into every beat by weighting the weak part of the preceding beat— cross-beat phrasing.[6] This tended to iron out the line and I felt strongly that it worked against the directness and angularity of the choral writing, undergirded of course by the hyperactive, square Alberti-like bass in the

Figure 3.1. Bach's *Johannes-Passion*, the turba chorus, "Lasset uns den nicht zer-teilen" ("the tear and rip chorus"), that sparked the philosophical disagreement between Flummerfelt and Robert Shaw. © Bärenreiter-Verlag Karl Vötterle GmbH & Co. KG. Used by permission.

orchestra [see figure 3.1]. I went up to him afterwards, and I said, "Robert, don't you think that phrasing works against the rip and tear and the confusion of gambling over the garment?" "No, not at all," was his answer. Almost immediately, something in my thinking shifted. And then I began to think more about this music and what made it work. I began to think about what off-beat phrasing does to the line, how it tends to flatten out the line, how it masks the natural "down-up," strong-weak alternation implicit in all binary rhythm. With respect to that *St. John* chorus, the sheer harmonic squareness of the writing over the likewise square but rhythmically boiling, Alberti bass is what so vividly symbolizes the meaning of the text. The biting, even harsh, verticality of the line helps evoke the meaning.

This experience then got me thinking a lot about the horizontal and vertical in musical lines and how the constant application of cross-beat/cross-bar phrasing inevitably dilutes the vertical directness and structural clarity needed in that piece. While there are many instances where cross-beat, cross-bar phrasing is exactly what the musical line needs, there are also many instances when a more vertical progress of the line is required. I also began to think about how overmarking a score can result in a kind of predetermined performance that strangles spontaneity.

Talk more about this and the difference one hears between Shaw's earlier and his later recordings.

His own fear of his gift seemed to increase as he grew older. When you hear the early recordings—those wonderful folk song recordings, and the spirituals, and the opera choruses on those old 78s, even his first B Minor Mass recording—there was a great vitality and earthiness, something elemental that was so special. That was Robert Shaw's genius. He generated an earthy sound that had shape and color and texture. It had line, and it had his innate rhythm, which was really a huge gift that he cultivated all his life. But somehow, as he grew older, his need to control every aspect of his performances continued to increase, and the compelling improvisatory gift you heard in his early recordings got stifled.[7] The New York critics wrote about this in his performances with the Westminster Summer Workshop chorus; they would almost always mention that the performance was too "metronomic." In fact, I once had a conversation with a well-known soprano who told me that in her coaching of a recitative with Robert, he said, "In the next three to four beats we accelerate from 62 to 65." And, this was a recitative—a free, speech-like mode of music!

As a beginning conductor, I accepted his rhythmic ideas and his penchant for unwavering tempo regularity. That came from Toscanini, with whom Shaw collaborated, and who strongly influenced his music-making. But then I began to consider that the heart doesn't beat like that, and, while tempo regularity is certainly needed in Baroque fugues, Classical allegros, marches, etc., there are many instances when the musical line needs much greater tempo flexibility—when a performance needs to feel more improvisatory. As I said earlier, I'm intrinsically an improvisatory creature, born out of my ability to improvise at the keyboard. As a result, my whole approach to music-making grows out of the belief that every performance, if it is to really work, should sound as if it were recreated at that moment. Hence, to the extent that you have predetermined it by virtue of how much you machined into it, you sabotage its capacity to be spontaneous in the moment. And, as you know, with Robert, as the years went on it became more and more predetermined. So finally for me in the last years, I just found Robert's music-making completely lacking in spontaneity and it didn't touch me. It felt dead.

Clarify why you think it died.

Because I think he was frightened of the powerful, almost volcanic, expressive intensity inside of him. His huge intelligence[8] and his obsession with order caused him, as the years went on, to distrust that powerful, elemental, potentially unruly force within.

For me, as his music became more and more refined, it became less and less communicative. I guess that's the way to say it. Also, when one rehearses on "doo doo doo" for too long,[9] the singers begin singing off the voice, and then the very core that keeps pitch centered leaves. In Robert's case, this particularly affected the sopranos—they did not, to my ears, always sound on top of the pitch. There was a kind of repressive dome on the sound. Also, continuing to count-sing for so long, while helping to build inner pulse, kept the singers from relating to the text, both with respect to meaning and to inflection. To be sure, the sound is refined. And the blend is impeccable. And the diction is impeccable, as is the rhythm. And it certainly has a force, because he was a force, there's no question about that. But I remember listening to him once, sitting in Carnegie Hall in the last years, and I thought, "If this man could ever fully embrace his huge gift . . ."

But this is a man who performed so many major choral works so often through-out his career. And, he was always studying them. Does it follow that, as one's concept becomes more cultivated, more refined, the more spontaneous imagining of earlier readings becomes squelched?

No, I don't think that necessarily follows. But if you get so obsessed with getting the rhythm right, with overcontrolling the tempo, with rubato too precisely calibrated, then you get trapped by your own rigor—maybe that's a way to say it. You get trapped by your own rigor because you can't, finally, in the moment of performance, let go of those things and be spontaneous. The constraints you have imposed upon your concept don't allow you to take risks in performance.

Now please don't misunderstand me. I am certainly not, in any way, advocating sloppiness in any aspect of performance. But I do believe that overmarking the score, attempting (so to speak) to machine-in every detail of the performance can, and often does, so straightjacket the singers—not to mention the conductor—that the freedom to be attuned to what comes in the moment is destroyed, and this stifles the living creative impulse that al-lows spontaneity to happen. At a certain point, you have to let go and trust that the technical aspects will hold. You need to just let it sing and, in a very real sense, to let the performance evolve organically and spontaneously.

NOTES

1. George Szell, 1897 (Budapest) to 1970 (Cleveland), is best known for his long tenure conducting the Cleveland Orchestra (1946–1970), with which he re-corded most of the great works of the Western canon. In Cleveland he developed a virtuoso orchestra with hitherto unheard rhythmic precision, clarity, balance, and transparency—characteristics that were to influence Shaw and, through Shaw, America's choral conductors.

2. The Robert Shaw Chorale was formed in 1948 and toured for twenty years, often representing the U.S. State Department on trips to the Middle East, Latin America, and the Soviet Union. Shaw commissioned works for the group from the leading composers of the day: Benjamin Britten, Darius Milhaud, Aaron Copland, Béla Bartók, to name a few. The chorale made many recordings, including the popular series *The Many Moods of Christmas*.

3. Arthur Honegger, 1892 (La Havre, France) to 1955 (Paris), was one of "*Les Six*"—a group of composers working in France whose music was seen as a reac-tion against Wagner and Impressionism. His most famous work, *Pacific 231*, depicts

the movement of a steam locomotive in characteristic pulsing rhythms and vibrant orchestral sonorities. His oratorios, *Jeanne d'Arc au bûcher* and *Le Roi David,* are often sung today.

4. Polish composer Krzysztof Penderecki, b. 1933 (Debica). The compositions of his experimental period greatly influenced a generation of composers. His major works include *Threnody to the Victims of Hiroshima* (1959 UNESCO Prize); *St. Luke Passion* (1966), commissioned by the West German Radio in Cologne to celebrate the seven hundredth anniversary of the Munster Cathedral; and *Magnificat* (1994), written to celebrate the twelfth centenary of the Salzburg Cathedral. Of his changing styles, he has said, "My *Threnody* is still avant-garde, but the age of experimentation is over. We discovered everything!"

5. Summer Session at Westminster dates back to John Finley Williamson, who ran it as a private enterprise and continued to do so after his retirement. Charles Schisler, dean of the college from 1975 to 1988, brought the idea under the Westminster umbrella and expanded it to include course offerings in education, church music, organ music, and choral conducting. For many years the summer choir was the centerpiece of Summer Session, with Shaw, and later Flummerfelt, conducting weeks of rehearsals leading to a performance of a major work. Schisler became a trusted colleague of Shaw and moved in 1988 to Emory University in Atlanta to head the newly established Robert Shaw Institute (also with summer choral seminars, near Shaw's house in Quercy, France).

6. Joe refers here to the chorus "Lasset uns den nicht zerteilen" (No. 54: "Lasset uns den nicht zerteilen, sondern darum losen, wes er sein soll" [Let us not rend it, but cast lots for it, whose it shall be]), a violent, tearing chorus. Shaw approached these choruses using a cross-bar phrasing in which the "and" of each beat is emphasized, as opposed to the initial part of the beat. Thus, while the syncopation and rhythmic structure is highlighted, the inflection is opposite that implied by the text (Las-SET uns DEN nicht ZER-teil . . .).

7. For a comparison of Shaw's evolving approach to sound, discussed here, consider *Beloved Hymns* (1945, RCA Victory Chorale), and *Evocation of the Spirit* (1995, Robert Shaw Festival Singers, Telarc).

8. The son and grandson of preachers, Shaw graduated in 1938 from Pomona College in Claremont, California, where he studied philosophy, literature, and religion and, later in his studies there, directed the glee club.

9. Shaw often instilled rhythmic energy and contrapuntal clarity through count-singing, a rehearsal tool in which the chorus sings counting a constant subdivision of the beats (e.g., 1 + 2 + tee + 4 +, replacing "3" with "tee" as the "thr" tends to cause dragging and is less precise). At times, Shaw's choirs would rehearse for hours count-singing contrapuntal passages such as the "Die Erlöseten des Herrn" fugue of Brahms's *Requiem,* sometimes exchanging "1 e + a, 2 e + a" with "do be do be do be do be."

4

MENOTTI AND SPOLETO

———— ∞∞∞ ————

We've already talked about your move to Florida State from DePauw, and about your first invitation from Shaw, to conduct Harvest Home Chorales *with the Atlanta Symphony. Talk about encountering Gian Carlo Menotti at Florida State and your subsequent long-time involvement with the Spoleto festivals.*

Gian Carlo came to Florida State in the spring semester of 1970 to be in residence for twelve weeks. They were opening a new theater building, and he was brought down to direct *The Leper*,[1] one of his two straight plays.

Menotti made a planning trip to the FSU campus in the fall of 1969, and someone suggested he hear the choir. I was rehearsing a concert, which included the Verdi *Stabat Mater* and the Penderecki *Stabat Mater*. We were in the dress rehearsal when I became aware of someone standing on the floor in front of the stage. It was Menotti, who said, "What a great choir; you must come to Spoleto!" He had, unbeknownst to me, come into the hall to listen. At this point I was very flattered, but didn't think he was really serious.

The following spring he came to campus for his residency. The School of Music had a mini music festival every year—a weekend of concerts devoted to one twentieth-century composer—and we had decided that year to do a Menotti festival. The opera department did *Help, Help, the Globolinks* and *The Old Maid and the Thief.* I conducted the FSU Chamber Choir and a small chamber orchestra in a performance of *The Unicorn, the Gorgon, and the Manticore* with the dance department. Menotti came to the concert and afterwards came backstage and said, "That's the most beautiful performance

33

I've heard of this work. You really must come to Spoleto." And I said to myself, "I think he really means it." The invitation was then official and created quite a stir, not only in the School of Music, but throughout the university and the Tallahassee community. The university agreed to pay the costs to fly us to the festival, and before we left, the Tallahassee newspaper devoted an editorial to the trip. Thus, in the summer of 1971, the Florida State University Singers traveled to Italy to be the resident chorus for the festival. I recall that many members of the board and the New York staff could not imagine why Gian Carlo would invite a choir from Florida that they had never heard of to be the chorus for *Boris Godunov*, which was the principal opera that summer. Happily, our work in the festival was very successful and all doubts were assuaged.

That summer, in addition to preparing the FSU Singers for *Boris*, I conducted performances of Haydn's *Lord Nelson Mass* and, as I mentioned, Dallapiccola's *Canti di Prigionia*. At the end of that first festival, I had a moment I will never forget. I went up to Palazzo Campello,[2] where Gian Carlo lived, with a poster for him to sign. He wrote, "To dear Joe, the new pillar of the festival." And that's when I knew I would be returning as the first permanent *maestro del coro* of the festival. The following fall I went to Westminster and the next summer I took the Westminster Choir to Spoleto for the first time, and the rest is history. That's how it all began.

Talk about Menotti.

Gosh, I think he was one of the most gifted men in lyric theater of our time. He was a genius—an authentic genius, no question about it. *Amahl and the Night Visitors* is a work of genius. I think that also of *The Consul*, and maybe *The Saint of Bleecker Street*.

His founding of the Spoleto Festival was certainly, a major contribution—first to the cultural life of Italy, and later to that of the United States. His vision was to create a festival that included not only opera, but chamber music, theater, dance, orchestral and choral concerts, while also exhibiting the works of major painters and sculptors. So many of the most significant figures in the arts were his friends. Jerome Robbins,[3] the great choreographer, played a large role in the life of the Italian festival. Luchino Visconti,[4] the great director, directed several operas. The Italian festival, and later, Spoleto USA in Charleston, launched the careers of so many major performing artists. There are legions of people he discovered. For example, the brilliant conductor, Thomas Schippers,[5] then relatively unknown, opened the first festival. Gian Carlo found Charles Wadsworth,[6] then a young pianist in New York, and asked him to establish a chamber music series. As in so many cases, that invitation became a springboard for him and, some years later, Charles would become the founding director of the Chamber Music Society of Lincoln Center. Out of that came Tully Hall because Alice Tully,[7] who was a friend of Gian Carlo's, was a regular at the festivals, and was the benefactress of the chamber music series.

Charles Wadsworth's Spoleto chamber music concerts included the likes of Yo-Yo Ma, Emmanuel Ax, Richard Goode, Peter Serkin, and Paula Robison[8]—then young performers just beginning their careers. My first summer I conducted some Schubert songs for male chorus, piano, and mezzo-soprano with Charles at the piano and the young Frederica von Stade as soloist. In the middle seventies Thomas Schippers brought an un-known young schoolteacher from Cincinnati to sing the Brahms Requiem. Her name was Kathleen Battle.

As I said before, Jerry Robbins was a regular visitor and contributor to the festival, and Luchino Visconti directed several operas. In fact, one of the most memorable operatic experiences of my twenty-three years in Italy was a brilliant production of Puccini's *Manon Lescaut*, directed by Visconti and conducted by Thomas Schippers. The list goes on and on. Henry Moore[9] designed the *Don Giovanni*. There is a Calder[10] stabile in front of the train station, a Buckminster Fuller[11] dome near town; even Isamu Noguchi[12] was a frequent visitor. I had dinner with the likes of Baryshnikov, Nureyev, and Willem de Kooning.[13] Zeffirelli[14] came several times to work. Then there were the writers: Ezra Pound, Stephen Spender, and so on.

Talk about the founding of the American Spoleto Festival.

Spoleto USA was certainly a huge gift to the cultural life of Charles-ton, and to the country as a whole. Reviewing the first festival, Paul Hume of the *Washington Post* called Spoleto USA the most comprehensive arts festival in the U.S. Spoleto USA in Charleston was, from the beginning, a vibrant panoply of artistic events, with the same range of offerings as the earlier years of the Italian festival. Like the festival in Italy, many artists, now giants in their fields, have had their beginnings at Spoleto USA. For example, Scott and Paula Nickrenz,[15] who directed the chamber music concerts from 1978 to 1994, brought a teenage violin prodigy from Bloom-ington, Indiana to play. That was Joshua Bell. Renée Fleming, before she was world famous, was a brilliant Countess in *The Marriage of Figaro*. That's just two examples of how the Spoleto festivals helped to launch the careers of so many who went on to become giants in the field. Now, well over thirty years later, the Charleston Spoleto festival remains a vibrant seventeen-day feast of the arts. Rising young stars still come to perform and to appear in the operas. All of the major dance companies have been there. Cutting-edge events happen alongside more traditional ones. It is a glorious happening to be a part of.

Gian Carlo had so many gifts, yet somehow what they promised were not, in the end, fulfilled.

Yes, Gian Carlo was also a great stage director, though his lack of self-discipline often sabotaged his work. I remember a *Boris Godunov* rehearsal in Spoleto in 1971. Gian Carlo was blocking some scene, and Christopher Keene,[16] who was conducting, came over to me and said, "You know, he has no idea what happens in the next scene." He was being a little facetious, but, as you know from very vivid experience, Gian Carlo's work was all so improvised, so invented on the spot—often invented with great brilliance, but sometimes without much forethought.

Gian Carlo's tragedy was that he allowed himself to be sidetracked by the grand life—or really, by anything capturing his attention—and, as you know, the machinations of his adopted son, Francis,[17] caused him to leave the Charleston festival in 1993 and ultimately brought down the Italian festival.[18]

In any case, Gian Carlo was enormously important in my life, and I cared for him, but I grew to not respect him. It's very sad—"To this we've come"[19]—that such an extraordinary gift had to come to this in his twilight years; very sad, because there might have been his *Otello*, there might have been his *Falstaff*. Maybe it wouldn't have been *The Rake's Progress*, a *Wozzeck*, or a *Lulu*, but it might have been an extraordinary gift to the world of twentieth-century opera. But, after those middle years, the quality of his operas significantly diminished. And much of this was due to the influence of his adopted son. Just tragic.

But, Spoleto changed my life. Remember, I grew up in Indiana; I was pretty provincial. By 1971 I had worked with Robert Shaw, but Spoleto opened so many worlds to me: being in the middle of all that, giving all those concerts, preparing all those operas. It was an amazing experience. And, it was affirming, too—to find an environment in which I could thrive and exist with colleagues and artists of that stature.

Name some significant Italian Spoleto Festival experiences.

In terms of musical experiences: the *Manon Lescaut* I mentioned. A Mozart *Requiem* that I conducted in the Duomo. Certainly the friendship with Samuel Barber. I had the chance to meet so many legendary figures in the arts. My first summer there I was conducting Bach chorales in front of the Duomo,[20] and looked up at Gian Carlo's house to see this Verdi-esque face framed in the window. It was Ezra Pound. Then there were the marathon concerts with Lukas Foss,[21] five-hour concerts, usually devoted to the work of one composer. There was a Beethoven marathon, a Mozart marathon, and a Baroque marathon. Lukas conducted the orchestral music and I conducted the choral portions.

And, all of the Duomo choral/orchestral concerts. You know, after our first year I insisted that our big choral/orchestral concert be in the Duomo and that it be free. I did so because most of the townspeople of Spoleto couldn't afford to come to the festival events. And every year I was sure nobody would come, but people just jammed the place. They sat in the confessionals, sat on the floor, and stood all over. They seemed to find some kind of sustenance in what we did—all the landladies, the people from the town, Jerry Robbins standing on one side, listening, Gian Carlo sitting in the front row, and Sam Barber sitting further back.

I stood at one concert with Allen Ginsberg on my one side and Jean-Yves Thibaudet on the other.

Those concerts were very moving for me. I was always so touched by the response of the people, especially the *Spoletini*—the townspeople—who loved the choir and knew them well from housing them, but could only afford to attend that one free festival concert.

Charleston experiences?

Well, certainly the opening year—1977; to be a part of the launching was unbelievably exciting. And it was such a huge success.

Every year the two Westminster Choir concerts have been sold out. The choir has, from the beginning, been warmly embraced by the Charleston community. I especially remember a Verdi *Requiem* and a Brahms *Requiem*. I conducted Renée Fleming's first choral/orchestral concert—Mozart's

Coronation Mass. I remember during the coaching she said, "I've never done anything like this before." Needless to say, her performance was extraordinary. We all thought she was great, of course, but who could have known she was going to have such a huge career. In 2005 Jennifer Larmore, who had first come to the festival as a member of the Westminster Choir and went on to have a major career, returned to perform the Mozart Mass in C Minor with us. Her presence in this concert was very moving to me, and an inspiration to the singers in the choir.

What operas? It's hard to say. There were so many amazing experiences. There was a beautiful *Parsifal*, which Gian Carlo directed. A stunning *Fidelio*. A wonderful performance of Gian Carlo's *The Saint of Bleecker Street*. A fascinating staging of *Madame Butterfly* by Ken Russell.[22] And so many others. Another highlight was our performance of Menotti's *The Unicorn, the Gorgon, and the Manticore* with a visiting dance company. It such a success that we had to add a performance. That was especially memorable because it was that work that had brought me to the festival in the first place.

NOTES

1. Menotti wrote the libretti for all of his operas, as well as for Barber's *Vanessa* and the reworking of Barber's *Antony and Cleopatra*. Despite these successes, his plays remain unpublished: *A Copy of Madame Aupic* (1947) is a drawing-room comedy in the style of Noel Coward, and *The Leper* (1970) is a straight play about the need for a minority to find a way to live within the limitations of the majority. (The Florida State performance must have been a U.S. premiere, but there is no way of being certain of this.) *The Leper* was presented at Spoleto USA in 1982.

2. The grandest of Spoleto family residences, Palazzo Campello (c. 1600) was rented as Menotti's home during the Spoleto Festival. It is Spoleto's singular surviving example of such a palace, with its enormous walled garden overlooking Spoleto's signature landmark, the ancient aqueduct Ponte delle Torri.

3. Jerome Robbins (born Jerome Rabinowitz), 1918 (New York City) to 1998 (New York City), originally danced in musical theater, then turned to ballet as a soloist with Ballet Theatre (to become ABT) in the early 1940s where he created his legendary *Fancy Free* (1944). He created dances for classical ballet and music theater and is best known for staging *On the Town, Call Me Madam, The King and I, A Funny Thing Happened on the Way to the Forum, West Side Story*, and *Fiddler on the Roof*.

4. Italian director Luchino Visconti, 1906 (Milan) to 1976 (Rome); his notable films include *The Stranger, Senso, La Terra trema, The Damned*, and *Death in Ven-*

ice. He directed opera at at La Scala and at Covent Garden and his production of Verdi's *Macbeth* opened the first Spoleto Festival in 1958; he returned there for a renowned *Manon Lescaut.*

5. American conductor Thomas Schippers, 1930 (Kalamazoo, Michigan) to 1977 (New York), studied at the Curtis Institute and the Juilliard School and debuted with New York City Opera at age 21. With Gian Carlo Menotti (whose works he often conducted), Schippers founded the Spoleto Festival in Italy in 1958 and was its music director until shortly before his untimely death. He was music director of the Cincinnati Symphony Orchestra (1970–1977).

6. American pianist Charles Wadsworth, b. 1929 (Newnan, Georgia), created the Chamber Music Series at Gian Carlo Menotti's Il Festival dei Due Mondi in 1960 and for Spoleto USA in 1977. In 1969, at the request of William Schuman, he formed the Chamber Music Society at Lincoln Center (chaired by Alice Tully).

7. After studying voice in Paris, Alice Tully, 1902 (Corning, New York) to 1993 (New York), made her debut in 1927 with the Pasdeloup Orchestra. After the death of her grandfather in 1958, she inherited his estate and became a benefactress to composers and art institutions, including the concert hall in New York that bears her name. The Spoleto Festivals benefited enormously from her patronage, and she was a good friend to Gian Carlo Menotti.

8. A flute virtuoso, Paula Robison cofounded the Chamber Music Society of Lincoln Center and was codirector of chamber music at the Spoleto Festivals with her husband Scott Nickrenz. She has commissioned works from Toru Takemitsu, Oliver Knussen, Alberto Ginastera, Elliot Carter, and Keith Jarrett. Since 1991, Robison has taught at the New England Conservatory of Music.

9. Henry Moore, 1898 (Castleford, West Yorkshire) to 1986 (Much Hadham), won the international sculpture prize at the 1948 Venice Biennale, inspiring commissions from all over the world (primarily large works for public spaces). His reclining nudes resemble landscapes and horizons; this was the style of the 1967 Spoleto production of *Don Giovanni,* conducted by Thomas Schippers and directed by Gian Carlo Menotti.

10. Alexander Calder, 1898 (Lawnton, Pennsylvania) to 1976 (New York City), is credited as the inventor of a new idiom of kinetic art: the mobile. His signature sculpting style—enormous, sweeping, metal sculptures—may be seen throughout the world, most notably in Chicago, Philadelphia, and Spoleto, Italy, where his stabile *Teodelapio* stands outside the train station.

11. American architect and author Buckminster Fuller, 1895 (Milton, Massachusetts) to 1983 (Los Angeles), devoted his life to identifying what he could do to improve humanity's condition. He wrote over thirty books, and coined such terms as "Spaceship Earth," "ephemeralization," and "synergetics." He was instrumental in developing the geodesic dome. Menotti brought a Fuller dome to Spoleto in 1967 for performances; called *Spoletosphere,* it remained until 2006.

12. Isamu Noguchi (Born Isamu Gilmour), 1904 (Los Angeles) to 1988 (New York City), began as a sculptor; his work is an amalgamation of Eastern and Western

elements, reflecting his multicultural roots. He mastered the ancient skills of the Gifu lantern makers and adapted them to electric lighting in his *Akari* light sculptures. He designed many stage sets for Martha Graham, including *Cave of the Heart* (1946, music of Barber), *Into the Maze* (1947, music of Menotti), *Hérodiade* (1944, music of Hindemith), and *Appalachian Spring* (1944, music of Copland).

13. Dutch painter Willem de Kooning, 1904 (Rotterdam) to 1997 (East Hampton, New York), emigrated to the United States in 1928 and became a leader among the American Abstract Expressionists. His wife Elaine was a highly influential artist and critic. He was one of many famous artists who created posters for Menotti's Italian Spoleto Festival; these included David Hockney, Joan Miró, Jean-Michel Folon, and Isamu Noguchi.

14. The many notable films of Italian director Franco Zeffirelli, b. 1923 (Florence), include *Romeo and Juliet* (1968), *Jesus of Nazareth* (1977), and *Tea with Mussolini* (1999). His famous opera productions include *Tosca* for Covent Garden and *La Bohème* for the Metropolitan Opera.

15. American violist Scott Nickrenz studied at the Curtis Institute of Music, then played in the Pittsburgh Symphony Orchestra. He was a founding member of the Lenox String Quartet. From 1978 to 2003, with wife Paula Robison, he directed chamber music at the Spoleto Festival in Italy and was instrumental in presenting many artists early in their careers.

16. American conductor Christopher Keene, 1946 (Berkeley, California) to 1995 (New York City), was music director at New York City Opera and Spoleto USA; the latter he helped found with Menotti, Charles Wadsworth, and Flummerfelt.

17. Francis "Chip" Menotti (Born Francis Phelan), b. 1938 (Philadelphia), was an aspiring actor and figure skater when he met Gian Carlo Menotti, with whom he spent the rest of the composer's life. He was adopted by the elder Menotti in the 1970s, then married Malinda Murphy (1960–2005), daughter of Margaretta "Happy" Rockefeller. They had two sons—Claudio (b. 1987) and Cosimo (b. 1991)—who were raised in Scotland. The elder Menotti named the younger director of Il Festival dei Due Mondi in Spoleto in the 1990s. The Menottis departed Spoleto USA due to tensions over Francis's role in that festival.

18. In 1993, an ongoing dispute with the board of directors of Spoleto USA (over their resistance to Menotti's insistence that his adopted son Francis assume a leadership role in the festival) led to Menotti leaving that festival. He made all Spoleto artists choose between Il Festival dei Due Mondi in Italy and Spoleto USA in Charleston and would not allow those working in Charleston to join him in Italy. Flummerfelt and Westminster Choir College continued their relationship with Charleston, and were thus banned from the Italian festival. Charleston has prospered, in part due to the return of general director Nigel Redden, who had departed several years before the 1993 rift (over a similar disagreement). The Italian festival subsequently declined over the course of fifteen years, amassing a great debt

and largely losing its audience; Francis was forced out of leadership in 2007 by the Italian minister of culture.

19. The words are Menotti's, as sung by Magda Sorel in her tragic climactic aria in *The Consul*:

> To this we've come: that men withhold the world from men. No ship nor shore for him who drowns at sea. No home nor grave for him who dies on land. To this we've come: that a man be born a stranger upon God's earth, that he be chosen without a chance for choice, that he be hunted without the hope of refuge. To this we've come; and you, you, too, shall weep.

20. The Westminster Choir sang impromptu, informal concerts of Bach's chorales, and, in later years, Renaissance motets and folksong arrangements, under the porch of Spoleto's Duomo. The complimentary acoustic of the portico projects the music out over the magnificent piazza, and into the homes nearby.

21. American composer and conductor Lukas Foss (Born Lukas Fuchs), 1922 (Berlin) to 2009 (New York City), moved to Paris in 1933 and settled in the United States in 1937 where his first piano teacher was Julius Herford. He studied composition at Yale with Hindemith and conducting at Tanglewood with Koussevitzky. He held music directorships at the orchestras of Milwaukee, Rochester, and Brooklyn. In 1953 he succeeded Schoenberg as professor of composition at University of California, Los Angeles.

22. English director Ken Russell, b. 1927 (Southampton) is best known for his (often controversial) films, notably *Women in Love* (Academy Award, 1968), *The Who's Tommy* (1975), and *Altered States* (1980). His 1993 production of *Butterfly* for Spoleto USA was set in the late 1930s in Nagasaki, where Butterfly is a prostitute; it ended with the bomb exploding over the city, followed by the illumination of Japanese corporate logos such as Sony and Honda.

II

PHILOSOPHY—THE CROSSING

5

SETTING THE SOUND

I'd like to talk about listening— listening, and sound—your experiences and ideas about both. On hearing your choirs, we immediately recognize them as yours. It has to do with the sound—the particular place from which the sound emanates.

The first thing that comes to mind is the fact that every conductor, by virtue of his or her psychophysical makeup, and the sum total of that person's life experiences, will create a sound that reflects the essential nature of that human being. For me, this begins with the breath. Breath as opening, as letting go, as the surrender to some inner source, an inner voice that will only speak if I am able to give up a kind of external control and allow an internal connection. At the core of this one must trust oneself and one's singers enough to be completely vulnerable. If this can happen, then there is a deep connection made with our singers that allows them to also open—to become vulnerable. Then there is a kind of gathering at the core of a creative impulse that is beyond the confining egos of both the conductor and the singers. This gathering at the core allows us to connect with the primal outcry—that longing which lives within each of us.

What's interesting is that I've heard the sound become "cleaner" in your choirs recently. Comparing today's sound to, say, the Folk Songs *recording[1] of 1981, you hear a difference.*

I'm not sure why that is. I'm not even aware of it. Maybe it's that, as we mature, we tend to move away from the raw, romantic intensity of our youth towards a more refined, perhaps more classical, approach to art. My own road as a conductor has certainly been the distance between what my ears wanted to hear—and that kept changing—and my capacity to realize that. Indeed, I didn't begin to make consistent musical sense to myself until I was in my forties. I suppose it's true that the soprano sound today is a bit leaner; maybe the whole sound is more so. Sometimes I feel I'm guilty of not letting voices sing as much as they should, in order to achieve greater clarity.

When you do Palestrina, clearly, you have the women sing straight tone . . .
I've never used that term. I just conduct it differently. More spin on the line. I get further ahead of the sound with my gesture. If you're ahead of the sound, the sound will tend to lean out. If you stay with the sound, it will tend to go deeper.

. . . and that's Brahms.
Yes, going deeper in the body and staying more with the sound. Concerning the Renaissance sound, I may say "steady the vibrato there," or, simply, "sustain that sound," but I hardly ever say "sing straight tone." I just don't like that sound. Excessive vibrato often results from a lack of vocal spin in the line. Especially with less-trained singers, there is often the tendency not to sustain through longer note values. If this happens within a line, it is very often because they are not singing a phrase; helping them, both verbally and especially gesturally, to understand the destination of the line, often helps to clear up an intrusive vibrato. Yet, I nearly always make the difference in sound through gesture rather than with what I say. And often, in earlier music, by conducting slightly ahead of the sound, it naturally leans itself out.

It's often been said of you that you pull the sound out of the singers—literally. It does sometimes look that way. And, you very often conduct with a cupped hand. Are you aware of that?
Well, I feel like the sound is in my hand. And I'm always shaping it—coloring it. What one does with one's hands, and with one's body, has a profound effect on the color of the sound. One's hands can even affect intonation, by changing or correcting the color of a certain vowel. For me, sound is a palpable thing, it's right in the center of my palm—like having

something that has substance in your hands. But, to pull it out? I don't think I ever pull it out. I hope it goes from my center to their center. That's not pulling it out, it's more a matter of releasing the sound. That's especially the case when the onset of the line is *legato*, or when the line needs to emerge gradually or very quietly. A perfect example of this is the cello line which opens the Verdi *Requiem*. Also the first utterance of *Requiem* by the men. To be sure, there are many times when the sound bursts forth and the gesture needs to impel the attack. For example, the opening chords of the *Dies irae* in the same work.

And your gesture . . .

Well, it's more than one's gesture. It's one's being; it's the way one breathes. It's about connection. Breath as opening. Breath as letting go of a certain kind of safe, external control. It is a surrender to a source beyond the constriction of one's ego. Implicit in all this is, of course, trust. Trusting one's self, trusting one's singers. Of course, in an instance like the Verdi *Dies irae,* the character of the breath impels the violent nature of the attack. It all begins with the breath.

NOTE

1. *Folk Songs: The Westminster Choir Sings Familiar American and British Folk Songs* (1981, Westminster Recording Division; re-released on CD, 1992, Gothic Records).

6

THE CROSSING

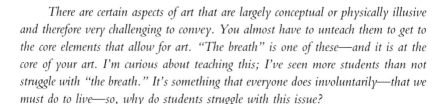

There are certain aspects of art that are largely conceptual or physically illusive and therefore very challenging to convey. You almost have to unteach them to get to the core elements that allow for art. "The breath" is one of these—and it is at the core of your art. I'm curious about teaching this; I've seen more students than not struggle with "the breath." It's something that everyone does involuntarily—that we must do to live—so, why do students struggle with this issue?

We all struggle with this issue, every one of us. As babies, we all breathe completely, we all open completely. Yet, for every one of us, the stresses and strains of growing up caused us to resort to mechanisms that protect us and that ostensibly keep us from being hurt. This inevitably results in breathing that is only partial. Of course, that is completely sufficient to sustain life, but it keeps us from opening up, from being completely vulnerable. I think the whole process of becoming more alive is a working through or a letting go of the fears that constrain us. At the core of this is becoming more grounded—more rooted—and breath is central to this. Most of us seem to be caught up in an ever-accelerating horizontal existence. We become diverted from being in the moment, by living in the past or in the future, thus not experiencing the full reality of each passing moment. Breath, in the fullest sense of the word, becomes a kind of vertical intersecting of this horizontal, historical continuum. So my belief that being fully alive, fully connected to a multidimensional embrace of life, happens at that crossing.

My experience as a conductor is: when I trust enough to breathe, to fully open my body, then that helps my singers breathe, it helps them to open, to connect, and that's when a group of individual singers converges. They come together in a place that is beyond any person, that is beyond my being, that is beyond each singer's being. Whether it's a creative impulse or a powerful spiritual connection—call it what you will. We've come together at the core, through the galvanizing force of breath, and then the ensemble is able to become fully connected. Implicit in this process is that this opening allows everyone to really listen. Indeed, I believe that only when we are fully connected, completely open, can we really hear. To be sure, someone with a good ear, even when disconnected, will be able to identify technical difficulties, especially issues of pitch, blend, and balance. But for me this is, as I have said, just the surface, and we can't fathom the meaning, the human/spiritual impulse, unless we are connected to our own center—so to speak, *the* center. We can't even feel the inner pulse because rhythm is a motor skill and therefore sits in the body. Any blockage that results from physically holding on won't allow us to feel or embody the rhythm. That blockage also keeps us disconnected from our solar plexus, the physical center from which all energy emanates.

Relate the "nexus" or "crossing" you just talked about to the intersection of—or balancing of—the cognitive and the intuitive.

Well, in this sense, I think of the horizontal as the cognitive and the vertical as the intuitive. Another way to talk about this is the cognitive as the technical—that which needs to be worked out and, in a certain sense, controlled—and the vertical as the intuitive—an opening to that which is beyond our control. This intersection, crossing, nexus, or whatever one chooses to call it, is the moment where spontaneity happens—when magic happens. Then our music-making is fueled by a source beyond our control. Suddenly we are conveying something musical that we never planned. Obviously, for this to happen, all of the externals need to be in place—all of the disciplines of pitch and rhythm. The tempo must be right, but even that may vary, depending upon the room or upon human factors. But when the technical aspects are in place and we are fully connected, then our music-making can reflect that wonderful balance of perfection and spontaneity we all live for. When that happens, everyone knows it, feels it, performers and listeners alike.

So, back to the crossing—the horizontal is where the music's been, and where it's going. The vertical—well, so many important thinkers have said, "The only reality is in the moment." So, it's not just about making music, it's a life principle. To be fully alive is to be—is to have the capacity to be—in the moment. I think that's what's at the core of all religions. I think that's what meditation is meant to bring about. I think that's the essence of prayer. Also, isn't that the purpose of meditation in Buddhism—to stop the chatter of the monkey mind, to be in the moment? Or, in a more universal sense, to surrender to a higher power?

In this context, talk about the balancing of action and reaction.

Well, that balance is central to fully functioning communication between two human beings as well as the communication between conductor and his or her singers or players. You can't communicate unless two things are in place: first, you are simultaneously open to all the information that is coming to you from the other person, and conversely, whatever you say and whatever information you send out, you do with complete freedom and without worrying about what the person thinks. That's the complete action, and the complete reaction. Indeed, it seems to me a fundamental life principle that for every action there is an immediate reaction— tension necessitates release, we breathe in, we breathe out, tides ebb and tides flow, night follows day, and so on. Now, the complete reaction can't happen unless you are grounded—you just cannot open. And, you can't act unless there is an instantaneous reaction. The parallels to conducting are the breath and the ictus. An ictus will not send out any energy unless there is an instantaneous reaction to the drop and to the beat. Think of the natural action/reaction of a bouncing ball. If you simply drop it, gravity pulls the ball down. The bounce is the natural reaction to the moment of impact. In conducting, any locking of the arm at the ictus creates vocal tension and the music that results is stiff and lacks resiliency and flexibility.

Very often the biggest challenge in teaching is getting the conductor to make an ictus. How do you get them to do that?

In my many years of teaching graduate students, I find that helping them experience the instantaneous, natural release from the drop of the ictus is very difficult. What so often happens is the grabbing I refer to above, which simply creates tension, and tension anywhere in the body—be it in the arm, the shoulder, the jaw, or wherever—blocks flow and completely obstructs the possibility of any flow of energy. One way to help a student let go of the grabbing and thus experience a natural rebound is to have them lunge at me as if they're going to stab me. They'll make a sheepish attempt to attack, but they grab before the thrust because they're afraid to completely let go, to really lunge. But, if they *do* let go with an uncontrolled thrust they will experience a natural rebound, a natural reaction, or, if you will, a reflex action. Further, within the beat pattern, wrist tension is the thing that most frequently blocks the release of energy. Any sport that requires projecting an object through the air demands a free and flexible wrist. If the wrist is locked, then there is no release of energy. Further, a conductor cannot influence the subtlest inflections of a phrase with a locked wrist. Tension anywhere in the body blocks flow.

Talk about the fear that constrains us.

Maybe it's partly inborn; maybe it's partly the product of our upbringing. But somehow, we all get trapped on one side or the other—on the intuitive side or the cognitive side—so that with all our life issues, we can't get things in balance. More people probably get trapped—and I believe that our culture is trapped—in the cognitive. Perhaps the power of scientific thought, and our obsession with technology, contribute to the notion that we can reach the ultimate truth in a linear fashion. Yet, a leap of faith is at the core of Christianity, and even great scientific discoveries, such as those of Einstein, involve a leap out of the linear continuum, and so forth. But our technical world has led us to believe that there is a linear path from here to there—from here to the truth. Well, I don't believe that. Only when that leap comes, and the light dawns, and the spirit speaks (or whatever you choose to call it), can real creation or re-creation happen. Musical masterworks emerge from what composers hear. To be sure, there must be technical mastery, but what creates an ongoing source of human/spiritual understanding is that the work grows out of a connection to a creative impulse beyond any human limitations.

Back to balance. My experience with many years of teaching, and also with dealing with my own issues, is that being overbalanced in a cognitive, technical approach to life, thus to conducting, results in a lack of flexibility, a lack of natural flow in the music we make. We become rigid, so to speak, and overgrounded. The opposite of that is to indulge in whims of the moment that are completely disconnected from the musical context. That simply results in structural incoherence.

You often begin graduate conducting students with Gregorian chant. Why?

Chant is a very useful teaching tool, as many students come to conducting so heavily influenced by the bar line. The bar line, as we understand it, and the control it has over rhythmic shape, entered into the compositional process after many centuries of singing chant. In conducting it, the gesture must be all about the most subtle inflection and seamless progress of melody. Chant is also a wonderful way to teach others how to manifest the organic inevitability of a line. Somehow one has to get to the point where one intuitively understands when a line or a phrase needs an impulse of energy, and when one needs to let go of the sound and allow the line to ebb naturally. For example, a cadence simply cannot find its complete quality of repose if we are still hanging onto the sound. So, often in conducting classes at Westminster I would say to a student when he or she was trying to control the ebb, the relaxation of a line, "Just let go of the sound." Instantly, the sound would become more luminous and the conductor was able to experience the line evolving organically. I'm pretty sure that's what Erich Leinsdorf meant when he said, "The art of conducting is knowing when not to conduct."

How do you create an environment in your classroom in which one feels safe enough to open up? What do you do in order for that to happen?

Yeah, that's tough. I'm not certain that I always do, though I always try to create a healthy, supportive atmosphere wherein people are willing to take risks. Maybe because it's not a question of doing it right or doing it wrong. I can show them, I can encourage them, I can suggest they try this or that to help them experience what I'm talking about. But it's never a question of right or wrong. It's always about process—each student connecting to his or her own inner voice. That is why I'm fundamentally opposed to teaching a "method" of conducting. Some wise person once said that a rigid adherence to a method can often serve as a crutch for the ungifted and a straightjacket for the gifted. Each human being has a distinctive psychophysical makeup, thus each person will evolve a gestural vocabulary that is unique. To be sure, the starting point for all conductors must be the internalization of all the basic gestural mechanics, beat patterns, etc. But then, getting to the heart of the matter, one needs to help students work through the fears that block them from connecting to their own inner voice, to their own sound. On a physical level, that means a teacher must be able to instantly pick up on any tension, any holding, any blockage. And I believe that tension is often rooted in the fear of opening, of being vulnerable—which I have already spoken about. Finally, of course, all so-called pedagogy must be related to the shape, the colors, and the human impulse of the music. So sometimes simply working with a student on a more poetic level can help liberate them gesturally.

Then there is the issue of a student who is afraid to take charge, or a student who is too self-important and is, therefore, overcontrolling. And, the funny things one resorts to . . . take a student who feels too self-important and, therefore, is not able to listen deeply—to open to and receive the sound—to stop overcontrolling. I may have that person conduct while sitting down, so that they are on the same level as the singers. Maybe even to close their eyes. Often, this will help them to receive the sound, to listen deeply, thus allowing a creative interaction with the singers. Or, with someone who is afraid to take charge, I might have that student conduct while standing on a piano bench. They may then begin to feel more important, and thus able to experience a feeling of greater command.

When teaching, you often talk about "when you hear yourself." I remember your saying, "When you really hear yourself it's going to scare the hell out of you." And you were right.

Well, I meant that when you are finally open to the voice that is inside you, and when someone finally connects to their innermost self—even for a moment—it can be very powerful. The whole atmosphere changes in the room; everybody knows that something is different, something feels different, but nobody quite knows what it is. I think they've gone to a place—a very fundamental human place—where they've never been before, but where, I believe, everyone longs to go, often without knowing it. When that does happen in class, it can be overwhelming.

Not infrequently, when a student connected with his or her innermost core for the first time, tears began to flow—maybe because they experienced a deeper level of sensitivity, or that they were able to touch a place deep within where they had been afraid to go. That moment of revelation, that's what it's all about. It's a kind of epiphany. And, that's also what helps create the atmosphere in the class; you can push a person, and exhort them to all sorts of things, and the whole class experiences what happens when everything finally works. They hear the sound, and they feel the difference in the room. They know that it's about something real, something authentic. It's about a connection that everybody longs for.

The extraordinary thing about the experience is that, once you begin to be able to find this "place," it becomes something that you don't think about.

Oh no, of course not. If you thought about it, you'd stop it, you'd strangle it, shut it off; it wouldn't work. You can't go there intentionally. Again, it's about releasing. It's about letting go. It's about surrendering to a source that, as I have said before, is beyond the limitations of one's ego. It's so much easier to stay outside—to be a kind of external controller—to always be listening for what's wrong, instead of expecting what's right. That brings me back to the issue of an obsession with technical perfection, which may produce impressive results but will never deeply communicate because it is disconnected from that human/spiritual creative impulse. The performance will have a kind of sterile objectivity, because no risk will have been taken, and thus nothing spontaneous will have happened.

What about those days when you can't go there and you don't know why, but you are aware that things are all screwed up?

You become very frustrated. When we come to a rehearsal or a performance with whatever personal baggage, we owe it to ourselves, to our singers, and to the composer to overcome that. But for me, the only way to unload that baggage is through the music. Whatever personal issues we brought into the room disappear and we become fully present, conductor and singers alike. Everyone is interconnected through the galvanizing power of the composer's voice.

And that's because the X and the Y, the horizontal and the vertical, are balanced. Let's delve deeper into the horizontal and vertical aspects of a musical line.

Years ago I began to perceive that many of us—certainly folks of my generation—grew up thinking that the movement of a musical line is always horizontal. We will tend, therefore, in our realization of a line, to mask or wash over those moments when, in fact, the line moves more vertically, when there is a quality of stasis in its progress, when the line simply needs to hover. The larger, stylistic consideration is the different balance of these two dimensions in Romantic works versus Classical works.

Though all generalizations are dangerous, we could say that the Romantic line is more horizontal; it may often grow out of infinity and recede into silence. (Consider how the Brahms *Requiem* begins and ends.) The shape of a Romantic line is less controlled by the bar line. And the human impulses that often drive it are ones of longing, of searching, of questioning, and of remembering. The Romantic line tends to dwell more in the realm of psychological time. That is, it moves counter to the regularity of onto-logical time. Romantic impulses are more subjective, more heart-driven. Therefore, implicit in all of the above is a line that is more horizontal in its progress.

Again, at the risk of overgeneralization, one could say that, at its core, the Classical line is more vertical, more controlled by the bar line. It will tend to move more in lockstep with ontological time and, therefore, its expressive impulses are more objective. In a Classical musical line, begin-nings, endings, and structural seams are much clearer.

The above is obviously painting stylistic differences with very broad strokes. Certainly, within Romantic works, there are times when the prog-ress of the line is more vertical and the reverse holds true for Classical works. Such things as the speed of the harmonic rhythm, the contrast of homoph-ony and polyphony, and certainly also the rhythmic dimension, contribute to whether the line proceeds more vertically or more horizontally.

All of the above is, finally, very difficult to talk about, because the considerations that contribute to the progress of a musical line are often so subtle, and to generalize as I have done tends to sound a bit simplistic. But I do believe that we must always ask the question, "Is the line more horizontal, or is it more vertical?" And then the full textural dimensions of a work become clearer.

Share some final thoughts about cognition/intuition as it relates to music-making.

Well, you've heard me talk about that Princeton psychologist Julian Jaynes, the Wada Test, and the book he wrote: *The Origin of Consciousness in the Breakdown of the Bicameral Mind.* It discusses why there are no longer any prophets, any oracles, and so on. As we have become ever more "en-trapped" in the cognitive, we have lost touch with that other side. I don't think he uses that word, but it's about that place where the voices of the prophets or the voices of the oracles come from. He describes the Wada Test, a procedure whereby the intuitive side of the brain is safely shut down—and the subject can speak, but can't sing.[1] And conversely, if the other side is shut down, the subject can sing but can't speak. *Now, to me, that speaks volumes.* And it's interesting that stroke victims who were musicians but who have lost the faculty of speech can sometimes form words by singing tunes.

For me that says it all. Music comes from the other side, from our intuitive side.

NOTE

1. The work of American author and teacher Julian Jaynes, 1920 (West Newton, Massachusetts) to 1997 (Charlottetown, Prince Edward Island), spanned psychology, anthropology, history, philosophy, religion, and literary studies. In *The Origin of Consciousness in the Breakdown of the Bicameral Mind* (Houghton Mifflin, 1976), Jaynes details that to which Joe refers:

> song, as we are presently discovering, is primarily a function of the right cerebral hemisphere. The evidence is various but consistent. It is common medical knowledge that many elderly patients who have suffered cerebral hemorrhages on the left hemisphere such that they cannot speak can still sing. The so-called Wada Test is sometimes performed in hospitals to find out a person's cerebral dominance. Sodium amytal is injected into the carotid artery on one side, putting the corresponding hemisphere under heavy sedation but leaving the other awake and alert. When the injection is made on the left side so that the right hemisphere is active, the person is unable to speak, but can still sing. When the injection is on the right so that only the left hemisphere is active, the person can speak but cannot sing. Electric stimulation on the right hemisphere in regions adjacent to the posterior temporal lobe, particularly in the anterior temporal lobe, often produces hallucinations of singing and music. (365)

Later, in "Consciousness and the Voices of the Mind," (*Canadian Psychology*, April 1986), Jaynes further explains his bicameral theory:

> The problem of consciousness and its corollary the mind body problem have been with us at least since Descartes. An approach to a solution to both may be begun by carefully analyzing consciousness into its component features and modes. It will then be seen that consciousness is based on language, in particular its ability to form metaphors and analogies. The result is that consciousness is not a biological genetic given, but a linguistic skill learned in human history. Previous to that transitional period, human volition consisted of hearing voices called gods, a relationship I am calling the bicameral mind.

III

PREPARING FOR
MAJOR CONDUCTORS

7

LEONARD BERNSTEIN

—∞∞—

Leonard Bernstein: A giant, who once called you "the greatest choral conductor in the world"—I know that embarrasses you, but it's a claim many wish we could make. You had incredible experiences with Bernstein, largely through your work with the New York Philharmonic where he was Conductor Emeritus by the time you began your work there. Over the years, you've shared many stories and impressions of the performances and recordings you did with him and I'd like to collect some of them. Let's start with that accidental meeting in Amsterdam when you took over the rehearsal of the chorus.

Well I didn't take it over; I ended up assisting him. In 1978, I was on sabbatical and in Amsterdam. I learned that Bernstein was rehearsing *Missa solemnis* with the Royal Concertgebouw Orchestra. So I called the orchestra and asked if I could attend some rehearsals. They said I could come that evening. It was Bernstein's last rehearsal with the chorus alone and was to be followed by a combined rehearsal with the orchestra. I got there just after the chorus rehearsal began and it quickly became apparent that things were not going well; Bernstein was becoming very frustrated. Soon after I got there, he turned around, saw me and said, "What are you doing here?" Then, during the break, he motioned to me to come up to the podium, and asked me to come to his dressing room. He called the *intendant* of the orchestra in and said, "This is Joe Flummerfelt, the greatest choral conductor in the world, and I want him to fix this choir." That's where that quote comes from. It was a quote that happened in the moment and now it has appeared far too often in too many publicity pieces. I wish it had been buried long since.

He wanted me to rehearse the chorus, and of course, I couldn't do that. The chorus didn't know who I was; it wouldn't have worked. He said, "Well, we've got to do something," so I suggested that he and I meet with the chorus director and that I would pass suggestions to the director through him.

What could you give him that was lacking in that situation?
Things like articulation to help clarify the rhythm, revoicing, and certain choral techniques to make the choir sound better. Bernstein sat between the chorus master and me and we talked through the score. He then scheduled another rehearsal with the chorus alone, and he had me sit behind him. From time to time he would turn around and ask if I had any other suggestions. I certainly couldn't tell Bernstein anything about Beethoven, but I could help him make the chorus sound better.

During my early years at Westminster the choir performed and recorded several works with Bernstein. He came to the campus often to rehearse the Symphonic Choir, which he loved. He always was very cordial, very collegial, and of course the performances were always exciting. What was always so clear was how deeply he had probed the essence of whatever works he was conducting. One might sometimes disagree with this or that musical decision, but whatever he did grew out of his passionate love of, and devotion to, the composer's work. Very often his reading of a work was a revelation, especially his performances of Mahler symphonies. Westminster Choir recorded the Second with him. The Choral Artists recorded the Third and also performed the Second with him near the end of his life; they were scheduled to record the Eighth with him the year he died.

As a young musician, Mahler was a mystery to me. But experiencing Mahler with Bernstein and the New York Philharmonic opened up that world to me.[1]

But what you learn from somebody like that, you can't define. I didn't have the kind of close relationship I had with Shaw. But, just collaborating with him on so many works was an ongoing learning experience. In addition to the Mahler performances, there were three Haydn masses, two of which were recorded—the *Harmoniemesse* and the *Lord Nelson Mass*. We performed and recorded Poulenc's *Gloria*. There were also performances of Liszt's *Psalm 13*, *Faust Symphony*, the Stravinsky *Symphony of Psalms*, the Stravinsky *Mass*, and Lukas Foss's *American Cantata*. For the Carnegie Hall celebration of the forty-fifth anniversary of his auspicious debut with the New York Philharmonic, Bernstein invited the Westminster Symphonic Choir to perform the *Chichester Psalms*—another amazing musical evening.

If you could say something to him now, what would it be?

I would simply say how deeply grateful I am that I had the privilege of working with you and learning from you.

He was also a great teacher, which, of course, so many of us experienced through his *Young People's Concerts* telecasts with the Philharmonic.[2] But what was a lesson for us all was to be in the presence of a man who, in all his genius, kept digging, kept growing. I got to watch him teach conducting at Tanglewood one summer. The clarity and the helpfulness of his penetrating criticism of the students were wonderful to witness. At Tanglewood I also heard him conduct a Shostakovich Fifth Symphony and the Tchaikovsky Fourth. Once again, his readings of these works, especially the well-known Tchaikovsky, were a revelation.

As you know, some people think he was overly flamboyant. I don't think so. For sure, he was larger than life and his ego was larger than life. But, somehow, I never felt that ego get in the way of his music-making. You could certainly say that some of his decisions were idiosyncratic. Those Haydn Masses we recorded with him—the fast parts were *really* fast and the *adagios* were *really* slow. But, then again, he could make those tempos work. Whatever work he conducted bore the stamp of a great artist for whom every performance was a re-creation. A man, who, with all his charisma, all of his accomplishments, never lost his reverence for the composer's work.

NOTES

1. Bernstein was in attendance at Tanglewood (summer home of the Boston Symphony Orchestra and Tanglewood Music Center in Stockbridge, Massachusetts) for fifty years, beginning in 1940—first as student of, then assistant to, Koussevitzky and the Boston Symphony Orchestra, then as conductor and teacher.

2. On January 18, 1958, two weeks after becoming music director of the New York Philharmonic, Bernstein conducted a *Young People's Concert*, the first of fifty-three live broadcasts spanning fourteen years. Originally broadcast on Saturday mornings, the programs were considered so important that for three years CBS presented them in prime time.

8

BOULEZ, MEHTA, EARLY
MUSIC, AND PREPARING

Those who sing with you regularly quickly come to think of rehearsals as a matter of digging ever deeper into a work of art in a sort of "closed community"—an intimate environment—prior to sharing the work with the public. The first step toward that public is the introduction of the orchestral conductor into the equation. Westminster, the New York Choral Artists, Spoleto, and the New York Philharmonic have brought you into contact with a procession of conductors that must stand as a singularly comprehensive resumé; listing those you have not known is actually easier than naming those you have. Let's talk about just a few that hold particular interest. First, Pierre Boulez.

Well, I began working with him in 1971, soon after he came to the Philharmonic. He is a phenomenal musician, and a very gracious man. When Boulez took over as music director of the Philharmonic there was a body of the standard symphonic repertoire that he had yet to perform. Westminster Symphonic Choir sang, I believe, his first Beethoven Ninth and his first *Missa solemnis.* Though the performances were technically polished, I didn't find them deeply satisfying. More rewarding were the big Berlioz works, such as *Damnation of Faust* and *Roméo et Juliette.* For one concert he paired the Berlioz *Te Deum* with Bartók's *Cantata Profana.* Because of his interest in twentieth-century music, I expected that to be an especially rewarding collaboration. For whatever reason, he had very little to say about the Bartók, what I believe to be one of the twentieth century's choral masterpieces. I think the only thing we recorded with Boulez was an obscure Wagner work, *Das Liebesmahl der Apostel.* It's a curious piece for triple male chorus with a complex texture and balance and intonation issues, which I was unable to overcome. Within the last few years the New York Choral Artists performed a Mahler Third with Boulez and the Vienna Philharmonic, and the Westminster Symphonic Choir performed Bartók's *Bluebeard's Castle* with the Cleveland Orchestra. Because of his consummate musicianship, Boulez brought amazing clarity and structural balance to these performances. As you know, he is today a favorite conductor of orchestras like the Berlin Philharmonic and is Conductor Emeritus at Chicago. Although his music is always supremely intelligent, for me it lacks a certain warmth. His huge musical brain is always in evidence, but his very reserved, rather private nature tends to keep the heart in check. Boulez is a wonderful human being, a man of great humility, and certainly a musician of extraordinary skill. Through his leadership of the new-music organization, the IRCAM in Paris, he's had a profound effect on the world of music.[1]

Zubin Mehta.

A very gifted conductor. My most satisfying collaborations with him were big, sprawling works like Mahler symphonies and the Schoenberg *Gurrelieder.* His capacity to internalize and to manage those big Schoenberg works was simply amazing.

Early in his tenure he conducted the Westminster Symphonic Choir and the Philharmonic in a wonderful Verdi *Requiem* that was, I think, the first choral/orchestral telecast in the *Live from Lincoln Center* series. Our first concert with him included a very lovely Schubert Mass in A-flat, and, some time later, a very moving *Elijah.* Sometimes, however, I have to say that his performances seemed a bit too facile and not deeply probing.

When it came to works written before the nineteenth century, I think Zubin was not so successful. I remember a *St. Matthew Passion* with the Choral Artists. Zubin asked for eighty singers, which is way too many for a group of professional singers performing Bach. But in our own rehearsals, I felt we were beginning to achieve a reasonable amount of textural clarity, and I had worked very hard on articulation and balance. When Zubin took over, he began to overdrive the sound. Instead of letting Bach's drama emerge on its own terms, he kept going for (what seemed to me to be) a more operatic approach. One night we came off stage after a performance in which the closing chorus of that great masterwork was really shouty. He turned to me and said, "That sort of sounded like Wagner, didn't it? And I said, "Yes, it did." So he did know that, in that instance, he was stylistically way out of bounds.

Those who know Zubin's operatic work, both as music director of the Maggio Musicale in Florence and of the Munich Opera, say that his greatest work is in that genre. There was, as you remember, also a highly acclaimed Ring Cycle, which he did with the Chicago Lyric Opera some years ago. Singers love to work with him and he is also a wonderful accompanist for instrumentalists.

Personally, Zubin is warm, compassionate, and a great humanitarian. He has a very close association with Pinchas Zukerman, Daniel Barenboim, and Itzhak Perlman. And he has been a great champion of Israeli causes, and is Music Director for Life of the Israel Philharmonic.

You mention the Bach. How do original instruments and the early-music movement affect your work?

Though I recognize the importance that an increased awareness of performance practices has had on the music before the nineteenth century, I have to say that my own romantic nature has caused me to not whole-heartedly embrace some of the influences of the movement.

I think that some performers, maybe because of a lack of trust in their own musical intuition, have allowed themselves to be guided by what some early-music specialists say one *ought* to do instead of following their own instincts. Of course, none of us embraces the inflated readings that earlier conductors brought to the works of Bach, Handel, and many others. Delving into the findings of musicologists and early music specialists does contribute to the refinement of our stylistic sensibility. Certainly, my own approach to Baroque and Classical articulation, phrasing, and scale of forces is very different than it would have been say, twenty years ago. Yet, I would far rather hear the old von Karajan recording of the B Minor Mass than recent performances with only one on a part, because, though stylistically it is not something that I would emulate today, it spoke from the heart and the soul of a great artist.

Although thorough scholarship is essential, I profoundly believe that one must, in the moment of performance, be guided by one's own intuitive passion for how a given work must speak, even if that results in a reading that an early-music specialist would say is not "correct." I think that is the trap that lots of academics fall into, getting far too caught up in what this or that treatise says one ought to do.

To be sure, there are many performers working in the early-music tradition that are exciting and engaging—Ton Koopman,[2] for example.

Twice, I prepared a *Messiah* for Nicholas McGegan,[3] which was very musical and very satisfying. I do, however, feel that many early-music specialists err on the side of faster tempi, and thus call attention to "look how fast and accurately we can play or sing such and such" instead of drawing the listener into what lies beneath the surface.

On the other hand, for me the realization of nineteenth-century works according to some early-music approaches falls very short. Some years ago the Choral Artists performed the Ninth Symphony with Roger Norrington[4] and his early-music players. Roger brought a lot of energy and a certain, rather frenetic excitement to his reading, but I found his slow movements to be far too metronomic and lacking in a natural, song-like flexibility. Also, his approach to Schiller's[5] text in the last movement was far from the cosmic embrace that I believe Beethoven symbolizes. This was especially true in the glorious all-embracing setting for the men of "Zeit umschlungen Millionen"; he asked for a kind of glee-club, stein-raising approach, thus making this cosmic moment sound very earthbound. The audience, mostly early-music aficionados, loved his performance, but I was simply unmoved. After the concert, I drove home and put on my Furtwängler[6] recording with the Berlin Philharmonic to feed my soul. It's not as technically precise as Roger's, but I think it had a whole lot more to do with Beethoven's spirit.

Recently there was a piece in the *New York Times* relating an uproar in England over Norrington's intention to play Elgar's *Pomp and Circumstance* without string vibrato. This makes no expressive sense and is, like a B Minor Mass with one on a part,[7] an example of the early-music movement gone a little crazy.

You have probably prepared performances for more conductors and more orchestras than anyone in our business. For all of those hundreds of preparations, how have you stayed engaged in the process when somebody else will conduct the performance?

First, let me talk about the process. In the putting together of a choral/orchestral performance, the choral conductor prepares his or her chorus independently, and the orchestra's conductor works with the orchestra alone. A few days before the performance, the orchestral conductor will have one rehearsal with the chorus, accompanied on the piano. From then on, the choir and orchestra are combined for the requisite number of rehearsals and performances, all of which are led by the orchestra's conductor.

In preparing for any conductor, I rehearse the work as if I'm going to conduct the performance. As a result, the preparation is grounded in a particular musical point of view. This creates the flexibility that allows the choir to adjust immediately to another conductor's musical intention. If you prepare a work according to what you think someone else wants to hear, then the result has no musical point of view, because it does not grow out of the preparer's musical understanding. It will also tend to be more rigid, less flexible, because the preparation has been constricted by a purely technical process rather than by an intuitive, organic one.

The core sound of your choirs always remains, regardless of who is conducting. Talk about this.

The sound is built in. It's embedded in the whole musical preparation of the piece. To be sure, each conductor will affect the sound, will influence the sound differently. But the essential core of the sound, which is grounded in the preparation, remains. Also important is that the rhythm is completely grounded. The ensemble then has its own heartbeat, its own deeply embodied inner rhythm. Then the ensemble can respond organically to another conductor's musical ideas.

NOTES

1. After several years of voluntary exile from France over disagreements with the government regarding arts funding, in 1969 Boulez was asked by President Georges Pompidou to create and direct *Institut de Recherche et de Coordination Acoustique/Musique* (IRCAM) and the cutting-edge contemporary music group, *Ensemble Inter-Contemporain* (which premiered his *Répons*). He presented their goals in 1974: "To bring science and art together in order to widen instrumentarium and rejuvenate musical language." Linked to the *Centre national d'art contemporain* at the Pompidou Center, IRCAM remains at the forefront of research and creative activities in contemporary, electronic, and computer-influenced music.

2. Dutch conductor Ton Koopman, b. 1944 (Zwolle), began as an organist and harpsichordist with focus on Baroque music. In 1979 he founded the Amsterdam Baroque Orchestra and in 1992 the Amsterdam Baroque Choir (now combined as one ensemble). He is a leading proponent in the authentic performance movement (using exact copies of historical instruments, for example), and specializes in the music of Bach.

3. British conductor, flautist, and harpsichordist Nicholas McGegan, b. 1950 (Hertfordshire), studied at Cambridge and Oxford. He is a leading advocate of

historically informed performances of Baroque music and has held appointments with San Francisco's Philharmonica Baroque Orchestra, the Milwaukee Symphony Orchestra, and the Saint Paul Chamber Orchestra.

4. Roger Norrington, b. 1934 (Oxford), has conducted most of the world's famous orchestras in earlier music. Reintroducing original instruments and practices, his London Classical Players (now the Orchestra of the Age of Enlightenment) received international acclaim for its recordings and performance of music spanning Haydn to Brahms.

5. Friedrich Schiller, 1759 (Marbach am Neckar) to 1805 (Weimar), author of Sturm und Drang verse and plays (including the historical dramas *Wallenstein, Maria Stuart*, and *Wilhelm Tell*), is best known for the simple poem that Beethoven set in the finale of his Ninth Symphony.

6. Wilhelm Furtwängler,1886 (Berlin) to 1954 (Baden-Baden), was director of the Leipzig Gewandhaus Orchestra, Berlin Philharmonic, Vienna Philharmonic, and Bayreuth, which he shared with Toscanini. He championed the music of Schoenberg, Bartók, and Hindemith, and he resigned his post at the Berlin Opera when the latter's opera *Mathis der Maler* (1934) was forbidden, though he remained in Germany through WWII.

7. Following on a controversial 1981 lecture given by Joshua Rifkin addressing OVPP (One Voice Per Part) in Bach, Andrew Parrot's book *The Essential Bach Choir* (2000) explores current theories on Bach's use of solo singers in concerted music, drawing on Bach's writings in the *Entwurff* (Bach's 1730 memorandum to Leipzig's Town Council entitled *Short but Most Necessary Draft for a Well-Appointed Church Music: With Certain Modest Reflections on the Decline of the Same*). Rifkin's own extended essay *Bach's Choral Ideal* (Dortmund, 2002) puts forth strong opinions about the use of solo singers throughout Bach's work. (An additional opinion is offered by Paul McCreesh and Martin Geck in "Bach's Art of Church Music and His Leipzig Performance Forces: Contradictions in the System," *Early Music*, November 2003.) To be fair, Rifkin concludes: "In the sense in which people commonly use it, we shall probably never discover Bach's 'choral ideal.' Bach, it seems clear, took his performance practices more or less as he found them but tried always to realize their maximum potential." Rifkin's performances and recordings attest to his conviction on this topic, with entire works sung one voice per part.

9

GIULINI, MASUR,
ABBADO, MUTI, LEVINE

There's no questioning the trusted relationships you've had with so many conducting colleagues. But, over the years, two seem to have made a particular impression, as if you were brothers or shared a common background. Talk about your special relationship with Carlo Maria Giulini and Kurt Masur.

Both were passionately devoted to probing the meaning of a work. The Giulini connection was short-lived but very special. In 1982, the Westminster Symphonic Choir was performing the Brahms *Requiem* with the Los Angeles Philharmonic. Giulini, who was then music director, sent a marked score (which very few conductors ever did) from which I prepared the choir. The time came for the piano rehearsal. Giulini was supposed to arrive on our campus at about four thirty; he had just two hours to rehearse, but, he was almost an hour late. His driver got lost.

I was so looking forward to working with this great musician, who was one of my idols. But because he was late, I was afraid that there wouldn't be enough time for him to make the piece his own. So he begins, and the choir sings the first "Selig." He turned and looked at me, and said "Ma, bravo." Then he goes on working and he's very happy with what he's hearing, but he doesn't have time to get through the piece. The next morning in New York we barely got through the piece in the orchestra run-through. But the performance was glorious. Afterwards we were walking backstage, and he said, "Come to my room." He put his arms on my shoulder, he looked at me and he said, "I don't remember when I've had an experience like that. I felt so spiritually, so humanly connected with what you created." And we'd just met. Needless to say, that was a very special moment in my life. When asked the question, "What are your most memorable collaborations," that evening always comes to mind.

And, the same kind of thing happened with Masur and the Brahms *Requiem*, when we performed it in New York with the Gewandhaus Orchestra. During the rehearsals he said something like, "You and Brahms must have been brothers," and I think I replied, "Yes, maybe I knew him in a past life." Then he asked me to bring the whole Symphonic Choir to Berlin, because he said, "I don't have a choir in Germany that can sing the *Requiem* like that." He wanted us to come for a performance to celebrate the 750th anniversary of the founding of Berlin. It didn't work out because of money, but that invitation obviously meant a lot to me.

Not long before that I'd spent a week with him in Leipzig, during a sabbatical leave. He had conducted Handel's *Ode to St. Cecilia* with the New York Philharmonic in 1985, and had worked with the Westminster Choir for the first time. He loved the choir, so I wrote to him after our performances saying that I was coming to Europe on sabbatical, and I asked if I could visit him in Leipzig. His response was a very welcoming yes, and he was unbelievably generous to me during my several days with him. He and his wife took me to Dresden. I had dinner with them in their home a couple of times. He arranged for me to go to Weimar. He connected me with the cantor of the Thomanerchor.[1] Of course I attended all of the orchestra rehearsals and performances. In short, he opened all the musical doors in Leipzig for me. It was the next year that he came to New York with the Gewandhaus to do the Brahms *Requiem*.

Little did I dream, or for that matter, did Masur, that not too many years later he would become music director of the New York Philharmonic, and we would collaborate on so many years of choral/orchestral performances. Like Giulini, Masur is passionate about meaning in music. Unlike Giulini, he could sometimes become pretty ferocious in the pursuit of the same, especially if he felt any lack of commitment to meaning on the part of singers or players. But it was always all about the music. He is a man of colossal human dimensions.

He demonstrated his passion for justice and human freedom in 1989 when a massive, antigovernment protest was taking place in Leipzig in the Karl Marx Platz where the Gewandhaus is located. The situation was very volatile and the *Stasi*—the East German police—were very likely on the verge of a violent response to the crowd, not unlike the explosion in Tiananmen Square in China that same year. Masur somehow got the governing principals, including the dictator of East Germany, inside the Gewandhaus, and was instrumental in defusing a situation that might have resulted in God knows what carnage. Needless to say, this speaks volumes about the character of the man. As you can imagine, the Beethoven Ninth, with Schiller's call for universal brotherhood, speaks powerfully to this man, and his many performances, often on New Year's Eve, were always memorable.

Another mountaintop evening with Masur was a Brahms *Requiem* we performed just days after 9/11. Traditionally the New York Philharmonic Orchestra opens its season with a gala concert, usually in later September. The day after 9/11 I got a call from the orchestra asking what we could do in place of the usual opening evening, which would, obviously, have been totally inappropriate. The New York Choral Artists had performed the Brahms with the orchestra the previous season. So, instead of the usual season opening, it was decided to have a benefit performance for the families of the victims. Of course, everyone involved contributed their services.

I scheduled a rehearsal for eighty members of the Choral Artists a day or two before the concert. We gathered in the large room on the tenth floor of the Rose Building at Lincoln Center. All of us were, obviously, in a state of shock, and all of us were so grateful to have this opportunity to contribute our talents in response to this horrific event.

None of us will ever forget that performance. Avery Fisher Hall was jammed. Before the concert, Mayor Giuliani said a few words, followed by Zarin Mehta,[2] the orchestra's president, who asked us to not applaud at the end. At the conclusion, Masur quietly lowered his hands and left the stage with the orchestra following in silence. You can imagine the impact of that performance and, at the end, the silence was palpable.

There never has been, I am sure in the history of this work—called by some a requiem for the living, with its sublime words of comfort—a performance so needed. Nor could there have been a more perfect musical offering to minister to the needs of the performers, those in the hall, and the countless who watched and heard it on television. Orchestra, singers, and conductor poured their hearts out in what, for everyone, may be one of the most powerful musical evenings of their lives.

There were, of course, many other wonderful collaborations—especially the major Bach works and also, interestingly, his brilliance with large-scale works of French composers. The Masur New York Philharmonic retrospective attests to that—a ten-CD set of works Masur selected from among the countless pieces he had conducted during his years as music director. He chose to include the *St. Matthew Passion,* Honegger's *Jeanne d'Arc, Missa solemnis,* the Debussy *Martyrdom of Saint Sébastien,* Ninth Symphony, and Stravinsky's *Persephone.* Near the end of his tenure as music director, he was interviewed on Charlie Rose.[3] Rose asked, "What are your most memorable experiences as music director?" He said, "Joe Flummerfelt and the choral performances." Of course, Charlie Rose had no idea who I was, or what he'd just said.

What is it? What is that thing between Guilini and you, Masur and you? Maybe I'm asking you to talk about things that can't be talked about.

I think it's because I responded to the human/spiritual dimension that Giulini brought and that Masur brings to music-making. Also, to their belief in music as a moral/ethical force that ministers to humanity on so many levels. Bernstein also brought that to his art.

Claudio Abbado?

He is a giant. Perhaps the greatest conductor working today. I've never worked with anyone who listens so intensely. He's so musical, yet one always senses a deep humility in his approach to the score and to his musicians. Many years ago Westminster Symphonic Choir performed the Ninth Symphony with him and the Vienna Philharmonic. That Beethoven was simply overwhelming. I've prepared the work countless times with numerous conductors and have recorded it twice, but that one with Abbado and the Vienna remains especially memorable.

Well, the third movement of the Ninth is the test, and they played so movingly.

Yes, he let it be, he let them play. He monitors with such intensity. I remember when he came to the campus to rehearse the Beethoven. How interested he was in what in what we had prepared. There was an amazing collaborative atmosphere in the room. He didn't impose, he invited, he guided. He provided this enormous musical embrace that allowed the composer's work to evolve on its own terms. It was always about the music, never about him.

Through the years I so often have said to my graduate conducting students, "You conduct with your ears." If your conception of a piece is embedded in your being and you really know it, then by listening at the deepest level, your hands will communicate your ideas in a very natural and expressive way. Abbado is the supreme example of this.

Near the end of my time at Westminster, the women of the Symphonic Choir sang Mahler 3 and the Debussy *Nocturnes* with Abbado and the Berlin Philharmonic. Along with the earlier Beethoven collaboration, these experiences with Abbado have remained at the pinnacle of my musical life.

Riccardo Muti.

Muti is a great musician. He has fantastic ears and a fabulous conducting technique. To hear him solfège whatever instrumental passage is unbelievable. However complex the line, however fast it goes, he never misses a note. He is passionate about getting to the heart of a composer and is always careful to use performing editions that reflect the latest scholarship.

Our first collaboration with him was a recording and performances of the Liszt *Faust Symphony* with his Philadelphia Orchestra. The Liszt is for men only, and during the recording session he came to me and asked "Are your women as good as your men? Because next year I'd like to do a concert performance of Verdi's *Macbeth*. You know, Verdi is my meat." And we did it, and it was a big success. And that was the beginning of many years of working together. During those years he programmed concert performances of many operas: *Orfeo*, *Pagliacci*, *Tosca*, *The Flying Dutchman*, *Macbeth*, and *Nabucco*, as well as a number of major choral/orchestral works. We recorded a Scriabin symphony, Berlioz's *Roméo et Juliette*—which was nominated for a Grammy—and the Ninth Symphony. As I mentioned earlier, we recorded *Pagliacci* and *Tosca*.

The *Pag* was with Pavarotti, who was known to learn a score by rote, and then that's the way he performed it; conductors were obliged to follow. Because Muti had such specific ideas about how pieces should be performed, I was curious to see how this collaboration of star conductor and star performer would work out. Before the first rehearsal I went to Muti and said, in a sort of playful manner, "So tell me, Riccardo, is this going to be *Pagliacci* according to Pavarotti or according to Muti?", and he said, with a twinkle his eye, "Is there any doubt?" And guess whose it was. Once Pavarotti had learned a role in a certain way, that's how it had to be performed.

Muti was always so collegial and he treated the choir with such respect. It was a special relationship. And after that *Macbeth* performance the Symphonic Choir was his choir of choice. In the closing weeks of his tenure as music director of the orchestra, there was a gala benefit concert for which Muti chose some of his favorite artists. On that evening he asked the Westminster Symphonic Choir to sing "Va pensiero" from *Nabucco*. Much to my amazement he also asked me to conduct the choir in "The Lord Bless You and Keep You" by Peter Lutkin,[4] the unofficial "school song" of Westminster Choir College. I was unsure how the members of the orchestra would react to this a cappella Christian benediction, but many appeared to be deeply touched. As you can imagine, Muti's reading of "Va pensiero" was magical. In our Carnegie Hall performance of *Nabucco*, some years earlier, his reading elicited such an audience response that we were obliged to repeat it. That evening, like so many others, was filled with wonderful music-making.

James Levine.

I've only worked a few times with him. Our first experience was performances of two Mahler symphonies with the New York Philharmonic over thirty years ago. The Symphonic Choir sang Mahler 2 one weekend and Mahler 8 the next as part of a Mahler cycle in Carnegie Hall that took place while Philharmonic Hall at Lincoln Center was being redone. I was enormously impressed with how gifted this man was. In 1979, at Zubin Mehta's request, I formed the New York Choral Artists; our first performance was Levine conducting the Philharmonic in the Stravinsky *Symphony of Psalms* and the Mozart C Minor Mass. Levine is a great musician. He's wonderful to work with, and his rapport with the singers and with the orchestra is so open, so generous—without a touch of arrogance. You never feel that James Levine is the Great Maestro. There are no histrionics; it's all about the music. More recently, I have heard him work with the Boston Symphony at Tanglewood, and he has certainly transformed that great orchestra.

Are there any conductors, living or dead, who you wish you had had the chance to work with?

Bruno Walter,[5] Otto Klemperer,[6] and Herbert von Karajan immediately come to mind. Bruno Walter had a long association with the Westminster Choir, beginning when he was music director of the New York Philharmonic. Alas, his last work with the choir was some years before I was on the scene. There is a profound nobility in Walter's music-making which I so wish I could have experienced in person.

Klemperer's music-making had such deep roots and such probing of the structural details along the way. I recall, as a young student in Philadelphia, coming across on old Vox recording of *Missa solemnis*, which he had done soon after the war. Neither the chorus nor the instrumental forces available to him at that time were very good. But the conception was overwhelming. As you know, near the end of his life, he again recorded the *Missa solemnis* and several other choral masterworks in London.

My first encounter with Karajan's music-making was the old Angel recording of the B Minor Mass, which I heard as a student at DePauw. I was so overcome that I ran around telling all my musical friends that they had to go listen to it. In the seventies I heard Karajan conduct two Brahms symphonies with the Berlin Philharmonic at Carnegie Hall. That was a life-changing evening for me. To hear that great orchestra live, and to witness the symbiotic relationship his gesture had to the sound, and the organic inevitability of his conception, completely blew me away.

In 1978, while on sabbatical, I was able to spend a week in Berlin as a guest of the Philharmonic, listening to his rehearsals and a performance. During that week I had the opportunity to be introduced to him. There was a handshake and simply the words "You are welcome." I shall never forget the look of smoldering intensity in his eyes.

NOTES

1. Thomanerchor is the large boy choir at Thomaskirche, one of the four Leipzig churches for which Bach was responsible from 1723 until his death. (It sang the premieres of many of his cantatas, as well as the *St. Matthew Passion*.) Today, the choir concentrates largely on the works of its eighteenth-century master.

2. American businessman and arts administrator, Zarin Mehta, b. 1938 (Bombay), has had a distinguished career as a music administrator with the Montreal Symphony, the Ravinia Festival, and the New York Philharmonic. He is the brother of conductor Zubin.

3. American television personality Charlie Rose, b. 1942 (Henderson, North Carolina), has hosted *Charlie Rose*, a nightly interview show on PBS, since 1991.

4. Conductor, composer, and educator Peter Lutkin, 1858 (Thompsonville, Wisconsin) to 1931 (Evanston, Illinois), trained in Europe and returned to Chicago to work in church music. He founded the School of Music at Northwestern University and was influential in founding the American Guild of Organists.

5. Bruno Walter, 1876 (Berlin) to 1962 (Los Angeles), was a protégé of Mahler and began his conducting career at the opera house in Breslau, Germany, then held

positions with the Vienna Court Opera, the Royal Bavarian Symphony in Munich, and the New York Philharmonic.

6. Otto Klemperer, 1885 (Breslau) to 1973 (Zürich), also began his career with the help of Gustav Mahler. He held conducting positions with orchestras throughout Germany, then fled to the United States in 1933 to avoid Nazi oppression and was later appointed music director of the Los Angeles Philharmonic.

IV

THOUGHTS ON COMPOSERS

10

STRAVINSKY

*I am always amazed at the ease with which we can switch from one com-
poser—or language, or style—to another, and carry a common thread of musical
understanding that traverses certain boundaries. Yet, as we grow and get to know
ourselves increasingly well through musical discovery, we realize that certain composers "speak our language" more than others; we seem to innately "get" them—they
take no effort. I feel this way about James MacMillan,[1] for example. For you, one
of those composing "intimates" is Stravinsky; you've mentioned many times that
not just Stravinsky's music but also his writing about music has influenced your
thoughts.*

Yes. His Harvard lectures, *The Poetics of Music*, his *Autobiography*, and
some of the earlier *Conversations with Robert Craft*,[2] I found to be very helpful in understanding his work.

Did you have contact with Stravinsky?

No. But I did with Robert Craft. The first time, he was conducting
the Stravinsky *Psalms* at the Philharmonic and he invited me to come to
the Stravinsky apartment to talk with him about the piece. Stravinsky had
died, but Mrs. Stravinsky[3] was still living there. In the course of our talk
he brought out Stravinsky's sketches. I held in my hand the yellow legal
pad that contained Stravinsky's very own sketches of the work. Can you
imagine how that felt?

As an aside, when I was in college, I remember listening to the complete works of Anton Webern that Craft recorded. And we are told that it

was when Craft introduced Stravinsky to Webern's works that Stravinsky began to apply the principals of dodecaphony. When I asked him about the Webern recording, Craft told me something very ironic. He replied, "Well you know I don't know why I ever got so interested in that music." But, he recorded all of it!

Then, sometime after we did the Stravinsky *Psalms* he invited me to conduct the music at Mrs. Stravinsky's funeral. The Choral Artists sang the "Credo," the "Pater noster," and the "Ave Maria" in the original Slavonic,[4] which had been sung at Stravinsky's funeral. The Russian Orthodox service itself was sung by the priests from a New York seminary. Shortly thereafter Craft asked the New York Choral Artists to record *Oedipus Rex*, *Requiem Canticles*, and the *Psalms*. He was recording all the Stravinsky works in a series for Musical Heritage Society with the Orchestra of St. Luke's.

That was really an unpleasant experience, because I found him to be arbitrary about the music. Clearly, he's got fabulous ears, but he created a lot of unnecessary tension in the rehearsals and I was very surprised that he sometimes made musical decisions that ran counter to Stravinsky's marking. One morning, during the recording of the *Psalms*, Craft was ignoring some dynamic marking, and I asked him if he didn't want the chorus to observe them more carefully. He made some glib response that suggested he didn't think whatever it was very important. Somehow he gave me the impression that he felt what he was asking for or not asking for was more important than what was in the score. This, from the man who had collaborated so closely with Stravinsky for so many years? Anyway, I found it to be a very unsatisfying experience.

⸎

You once told me that you'd like to go away to the woods with a chamber choir—great singers—and work on the Stravinsky Mass every day, until you got it right.

True. Once in a conducting class, I worked with one of the students for a very long time on the first few measures, just trying to get it perfectly in tune. Finding the exact color of every sonority revealed how sensitively Stravinsky symbolized that opening petition for mercy. I've only performed it once, in France, at the Colmar Festival,[5] a number of years ago with the Westminster Choir. Stravinsky's ear for sonority, his voicing, his economy of means, his structural clarity—are all qualities that attract me. Especially in the works of his middle, Neoclassical period. Concerning the "Credo" of the Mass—I remember, one morning, in Boulanger's class we were reading that movement. We had just sung the opening bars, and she stopped us and said, "No, no, no, it must be like it's carved out of stone"—meaning, I think, not inflected, very direct, very objective. For sure, the objectivity of his setting of the Mass contributes to its universality.

Stravinsky said some pretty outlandish things regarding the expressive nature of music. He could be, and often was very dogmatic. For example, when he said "Music can't express anything but an ordering of time."[6]

Do you believe it?

No. I don't believe it, absolutely not. Look at the primitive rhythmic drive in *The Rite of Spring*. And, how Stravinsky uses the structure to symbolize the text in the *Symphony of Psalms* and the way in which the opening choral wailing on two notes—E and F, always being drawn back to E, over the entrapment of an *ostinato*—symbolizes or expresses the entrapped human outcry of the text, "Exaudi orationem meam, Domine" (Hear my prayer, Lord, Psalm 38). Or how the melodic hovering of the choral fugue subject in the second movement so beautifully symbolizes the words "I waited patiently for the Lord." No, the powerful way Stravinsky uses structural devices to symbolize the text goes way beyond a simple ordering of time. This remark is clearly Stravinsky the Neoclassicist overreacting to what he considered the expressive excesses of the late nineteenth century.

It does seem to me, however, that in his post-Neoclassical period (as I mentioned, sparked by Craft's introducing him to the works of Webern) a lot of the expressive juice was drained from his compositions. For example, his *Requiem Canticles* do not interest me nearly as much as the Mass or the *Psalms* or *Oedipus Rex*.

When you prepare the Symphony of Psalms, *you sometimes talk about ontological time and its relationship to music.*

Well, that's a bigger issue than simply in Stravinsky. Earlier, when I was talking about the horizontal and the vertical in musical lines, I alluded to the relationship of a musical line to ontological time. Stravinsky says music either moves in tandem with or counter to ontological time.[7] That which moves in tandem with time tends to proceed from the principle of unity. And, although he didn't say this, I would add that he is describing a Classical, more objective relationship between sound and time. Conversely, that which moves counter to ontological time moves in the realm

Figure 10.1.   The section of Stravinsky's *Symphony of Psalms*: "This musical passage hovers in time and in space and the effect is spellbinding." © 1931 by Hawkes and Son (London) Ltd. Reprinted by permission of Boosey & Hawkes, Inc.

of the psychological and the subjective and, is therefore, a more Romantic relationship between sound and real time. As I said earlier, music that is in tandem with ontological or real time is more vertical whereas music that moves more in the realm of psychological time is more horizontal. With respect to the vertical it is important that the conductor stay with the sound. This is one of the hardest to teach conductors: to get them to stay with the sound—to stay in tandem with the sound and not always to be ahead of it. Staying with the sound requires the conductor to be more vulnerable and I think that conductors who are always ahead of the sound and then impose an unrelenting horizontal quality to the line do so because they are unable to be in the moment—afraid of the intimate connection to the sound, which that relationship demands.

So that is one of the difficult things about performing Stravinsky—especially those works from his Neoclassical period. The third movement of the *Psalms*, especially the closing section, is a perfect example of the musical line being in tandem with ontological time. It's as if all of humanity is joined together in an unending procession of praise which has entered another realm of time and motion. The atmosphere is almost Zen-like, hypnotic, and one feels that the eyes of every being are looking upward as the words of this universal psalm of praise are being sung [see figure 10.1].

For me this is a quintessential example of a musical line that proceeds vertically. This verticality is evoked so simply by the choral parts, each of which moves back and forth within a very narrow melodic compass, further reinforced by the static quality of the instrumental *ostinato*. This musical passage hovers in time and in space and the effect is spellbinding.

NOTES

1. James MacMillan, b. 1959 (Killwinning, Scotland), reached international fame through the BBC Symphony Orchestra's premiere of his *Confession of Isobel Gowdie* at the Proms in 1990. A prolific composer of choral music, much of his work springs from his devout Catholicism.

2. Robert Craft, b. 1923 (Kingston, New York), studied at the Juilliard School and championed early-seventeenth-century music and that of the Second Viennese School. His artistic partnership with Igor Stravinsky lasted thirty years and produced several books. He has conducted all of the major orchestras in the United States and recorded many works of Stravinsky, Schoenberg, Varèse, and Webern.

3. Of German noble descent, Vera de Bosset Soudeikine Stravinsky, 1892 to 1992 (New York), allegedly changed her name (from Vera Bosse) in France to hide her German lineage. She met Stravinsky in 1921 and left her husband shortly

thereafter to become Stravinsky's mistress. They married in 1940 after the death of his first wife.

4. Stravinsky set "Ave Maria" in two versions. The first, unaccompanied, in Slavonic, is notable for its extreme simplicity and Phrygian flavor (following the rules of his Russian Orthodox childhood). Stravinsky once stated, "I can endure unaccompanied singing in only the most harmonically primitive music." The second is a reworking of the first, in Latin, with an extension of some fifteen bars that include a final "Amen."

5. Princeton, New Jersey and Colmar, France have a cultural exchange relationship. It was the hope of Vladimir Spivakov, leader of the Moscow Virtuosi (the resident orchestra at Festival Internationale de Colmar) that a festival similar to the one in Colmar could take place in Princeton as well. The Westminster Choir was in residence at the Colmar Festival for only one summer.

6. "I consider that music, by its very nature, is essentially powerless to express anything at all, whether a feeling, an attitude of mind, a psychological mood, a phenomenon of nature, etc. . . . . Expression has never been an inherent part of music." Igor Stravinsky, *Chronicle of My Life* (London: Victor Gollancz, 1936).

In his *Poetics of Music in the Form of Six Lessons* (translated by Arthur Knodel and Ingolf Dahl; Cambridge, Mass: Harvard University Press, 1947), Stravinsky tempers and refines this idea:

> *Inspiration, art, artist*—so many words, hazy at least, that keep us from seeing clearly in a field where everything is balance and calculation through which the breath of the speculative spirit blows. It is afterwards, and only afterwards, that the emotive disturbance which is at the root of inspiration may arise—an emotive disturbance about which people talk so indelicately by conferring upon it a meaning that is shocking to us and that compromises the term itself. Is it not clear that this emotion is merely a reaction on the part of the creator grappling with that unknown entity which is still only the object of his creating and which is to become a work of art? Step by step, link by link, it will be granted him to discover the work. It is this chain of discoveries, as well as each individual discovery, that gives rise to the emotion—an almost physiological reflex, like that of the appetite causing a flow of saliva—this emotion which invariably follows closely the phases of the creative process. (51–52)

7. From Stravinsky's *Poetics of Music*:

> music is based on temporal succession and requires alertness of memory. Consequently music is a *chronologic* art, as painting is a *spatial* art. Music presupposes before all else a certain organization in time, a chrononomy—if you will permit me to use a neologism. (29)
>
> What gives the concept of musical time its special stamp is that this concept is born and develops as well outside of the categories of psychological time as it does simultaneously with them. All music, whether it submits to the normal flow of time, or whether it disassociates itself therefrom, establishes a particular relationship, a sort of

counterpoint between the passing of time, the music's own duration, and the material and technical means through which the music is made manifest. (32)

Music that is based on ontological time is generally dominated by the principle of similarity. The music that adheres to psychological time likes to proceed by contrast. To these two principles which dominate the creative process correspond the fundamental concepts of variety and unity. . . . For myself I have always considered that in general it is more satisfactory to proceed by similarity rather than by contrast. Music thus gains strength in the measure that it does not succumb to the seductions of variety. What it loses in questionable riches it gains in true solidity. . . . Contrast produces an immediate effect. Similarity satisfies us only in the long run. Contrast is an element of variety, but it divides our attention. Similarity is born of a striving for unity. The need to seek variety is perfectly legitimate, but we should not forget that the One precedes the Many. Moreover, the coexistence of art, like all possible problems for that matter, including the problem of knowledge and of Being, revolve ineluctably about this question, with Parmenides on one side denying the possibility of the Many and Heraclitus on the other denying the existence of the One. (33–34)

With Christopher Keene, Thomas Schippers, and a technician on the Piazza del Duomo, Spoleto, early 1970s. Photo from Foto De Furia, Spoleto.

Accepting the Pegasus d'Oro, Mobil Oil's top prize for artistic contribution to the Spoleto Festival, on stage of the Caio Melisso, Spoleto, with Gian Carlo Menotti and the president of Mobil Oil Italia, July 1975. Photo from Foto De Furia, Spoleto.

With Pierre Boulez, rehearsing in the Westminster Playhouse, 1977. Photo from Westminster Choir College of Rider University.

Rehearsing in Charleston, 1977.
Photo © William Struhs.

With Krzysztof Penderecki in the Playhouse, late 1970s. Photo from Westminster Choir College of Rider University.

With Gian Carlo Menotti and choreographer Salvatore Aiello at rehearsal of the composer's *The Unicorn, the Gorgon, and the Manticore*, Charleston, 1983. Photo © William Struhs.

Conducting the *Concerto in Piazza* at Il Festival dei Due Mondi with the Westminster Choir, Bel Canto Chorus of Milwaukee, Spoleto Festival Orchestra, and soloists (from left) Sylvia McNair, Katryn Cowdryck, Robert Grayson, and Philip Skinner. July 1983. Photo from Foto de Furia, Spoleto.

With Gian Carlo Menotti and longtime friends and Spoleto Festival colleagues Erika Gastelli and Carmen Kovens, Charleston, 1985. Photo: © William Struhs.

Conducting the annual *Concerto in Duomo*, Spoleto, 1985. Photo © William Struhs.

With Leonard Bernstein in an editing session. Photo from Westminster Choir College of Rider University.

With Leonard Bernstein and Lukas Foss on the Westminster Campus during rehearsals for Foss's *American Cantata*. Photo from Westminster Choir College of Rider University.

With Bernstein listening to playbacks in a recording session, late 1980s. Photo from Westminster Choir College of Rider University.

With Zubin Mehta in the Westminster Playhouse, 1982. Photo from Cliff Moore.

With Riccardo Muti signing autographs in the Westminster Playhouse, mid-1980s. Photo from Westminster Choir College of Rider University.

Rehearsing Mahler's Symphony no. 2 in the Westminster Playhouse. Photo from Westminster Choir College of Rider University.

With Riccardo Muti on the Westminster campus, late 1980s. Photo from Westminster Choir College of Rider University.

With Kurt Masur on the Westminster campus, c. 1987. Photo from Westminster Choir College of Rider University.

Honegger's *King David* at Spoleto USA, with the Westminster Choir, Spoleto Festival Orchestra, soloists (from left) Mark Thomsen, Margaret Cusack, and Mignon Dunn, and narrator E. G. Marshall. Charleston, 1987. Photo © William Struhs.

Rehearsal for *King David* with Spiros Argiris at the harmonium and Glenn Parker (longtime Westminster Choir accompanist) at the piano, Charleston, 1987. Photo © William Struhs.

With Bernstein at his second Musical America "Musician of the Year" party, New York, 1989. Photo from Westminster Choir College of Rider University.

With Spiros Argiris in Charleston, early 1990s. Photo © William Struhs.

Conducting at Carnegie Hall, 1992. Photo © Steve J. Sherman.

One of many formal Westminster Choir photos, c. 1993. Photo from Westminster Choir College of Rider University.

With Westminster alum Jennifer Larmore at Carnegie Hall's *Christmas with the Westminster Choir*, 1993. Photo © Steve J. Sherman.

With George Shearing at Carnegie Hall's *Christmas with the Westminster Choir,* 1994. Photo from Chris Lee.

With Kurt Masur and Nancianne Parrella, Westminster Choir's accompanist, in the Westminster Playhouse, 1995. Photo from Westminster Choir College of Rider University.

With Spoleto USA colleague Charles Wadsworth, Charleston, 1997. Photo © William Struhs.

Formal headshot by Don Hunstein.

Conducting at Spoleto USA, Charleston, early 2000s. Photo © William Struhs.

Conducting Westminster Choir at Spoleto USA, Charleston, 1987. Nally is third row center of the choir. Photo © William Struhs.

Congratulating composer Stephen Paulus after the premiere of his *Voices of Light* on stage at Avery Fisher Hall, New York City, April 12, 2001. Photo from Star-Ledger Photographs, 2001, *The Star-Ledger*, Newark.

11

BARBER, BRITTEN,
COPLAND, SCHOENBERG

I'm very envious of your experiences with Samuel Barber, who I never met; his music has always held a special place for me and I revere him for writing whatever he "heard"—for ignoring his critics and the quickly changing compositional trends of his time. I grew up near his hometown and when I later taught at the university there, I used to go out to his simple gravesite and talk to him. You had a close association with Barber—personally and musically—that began in Spoleto. What are your memories of him?

Even though by 1971 they were no longer together, Sam and Gian Carlo remained close friends, and Barber came to the festival in Italy every year. He also came to the opening years of the Charleston festival. I met him in that first 1971 summer, and we began to get acquainted, especially, I think, because he loved the Westminster Choir. He came to our rehearsals, and always to our performances. That meant the world to me. During those early summers there were many times when we talked about a range of musical matters. I do remember him talking about his opera, *Antony and Cleopatra*—not too many years after its premiere for the opening of the new Metropolitan Opera House at Lincoln Center. The critics responded to the work very harshly. He was really burned by that experience and said if he didn't have to maintain a certain lifestyle, he wouldn't compose another note of music. He was, at that time, writing some songs for Dietrich Fischer-Dieskau, for Charles Wadsworth's Lincoln Center Chamber Music Society.[1] Later Barber did revise *Antony and Cleopatra*, and the Westminster Choir was the chorus for Spoleto performances, both in Italy and in

Charleston. The Italian production was recorded, and that recording won a Grammy.[2]

I think Barber wrote some of the most beautiful music of any twentieth-century American composer. Westminster Choir has performed most of his choral works, and I especially love the *Reincarnations*, which I believe are the finest twentieth-century part songs by an American. I first approached his "Agnus Dei"—Barber's choral setting of his *Adagio for Strings*—late in my Westminster years; we took it on tour, and included it on our *Heaven to Earth* recording. I had always loved the *Adagio*, but was apprehensive about the choir's capacity to vocally sustain those long, long lines. Happily, the performances worked.

Personally, Barber was a very sensitive, caring man who tended to mask this behind a rather prickly exterior. He could be very critical, yet, especially in musical matters, his comments were often on the mark because of his enormous musical gifts, his penetrating intelligence, and his deeply cultured nature. As you know, in addition to being a major composer, he was a gifted singer and a fine pianist.

Not too long before he died, following a long illness, Sam had requested that the Westminster Choir sing at his funeral; I was deeply touched by this. He wanted us to sing the last madrigal from Gian Carlo's *The Unicorn, the Gorgon, and the Manticore*, which we did. He also had wanted "Anthony O'Daly" from his *Reincarnations*, but there simply wasn't enough time to do it justice. So, with Gian Carlo's blessing, we did Barber's "A Nun Takes the Veil." This was for his service in West Chester, Pennsylvania, where he grew up. I shall never forget that day, and how honored I felt to be a part of the remembrance of this great composer.

Talk about Benjamin Britten—another composer for whose works you also have a great affinity.

I do love Britten. I have performed many of his smaller works and have been a part of several performances of the *War Requiem*. Masur did it twice, once with the New York Choral Artists and once with the Westminster Symphonic Choir, which was recorded. The Symphonic Choir also performed it with Rostropovich conducting the Philharmonic, and with Sawallisch conducting the Philadelphia Orchestra.

What most interests me in Britten is his choice of texts and the beauty with which he sets them—for example, his poignant setting of Christopher Smart's[3] texts in *Rejoice in the Lamb*. You know that the Smart poem is a small volume, and Britten chose just the perfect verses for his small masterpiece. Think also of the sensitivity with which he chose the Wilfred Owen[4] antiwar poems for the *War Requiem*, and how he organized and related them to the liturgical Requiem texts. I came to love the *Requiem* slowly, and I'm not sure why. Some years ago I would have said that, in certain places Britten's brain seems to overtake his ear, resulting in passages that didn't seem to me very natural, though they were rigorously correct structurally. But I have grown past this, and believe that the *War Requiem* is one of the great choral masterworks of the twentieth century. For me the most moving moments come when, near the end of the work, the tenor, who symbolizes the Allied forces, and the baritone, symbolizing the Axis forces, have met, and the baritone sings, "I am the enemy you killed, my friend." The reconciliation is accomplished as the two sing the haunting, simple duet, "Let us sleep now," while the choral forces and the soprano solo sing the ravishing canonic setting of "In paradisum." It is a deeply moving moment and a masterstroke of musical symbolism.

Aaron Copland.

I conducted the Westminster Choir in performances of all of his nonorchestral choral works as part of the New York Philharmonic Copland Festival a few years ago. Yet, he's a composer with whom I don't feel a deep connection, though I certainly recognize that he has a unique American voice. The New York concerts included *In the Beginning*, and, though I found it interesting, I will never have the relationship to it that I have, say, with "Friede auf Erden," or the Poulenc Mass, or *Cantata Profana*, Ives' *Psalm 90*—to name a few significant twentieth-century choral works. I'm not sure why that is. Copland was certainly a major twentieth-century composer. The ballets are wonderful. Maybe it's because I don't sense a spiritual dimension in his choral works. I think the only sacred texts Copland set were those early motets written when he was a student of Boulanger. They're interesting, but, as I recall, he only considered them student pieces and never really wanted them to be published. Unlike Bernstein, for example, with his *Kaddish Symphony* or the *Chichester Psalms*, I don't think Copland set any sacred texts other than those motets. I think that is telling.

Well, we could speak for hours about the differences between the two, or even just on this issue of their choice of themes and texts, the Jewish influences on the

music of one and the curious absence of them in the other. Talk about "Friede auf Erden." A work you do have a deep connection to. What is your history with that piece?

I've always been fascinated with the piece. The Westminster Choir first performed it for a Schoenberg festival on the campus, and we also toured with it that year. Somewhat later, I performed it with the New York Choral Artists for a celebration of Bonhöffer's life and his connection to Union Seminary in New York.[5] Then, a few years ago, after hearing the Westminster Choir in the fall I thought, "This choir can do 'Friede auf Erden.'" So, we toured with it and included it on the *Heaven to Earth* recording. It is a profoundly spiritual work, beginning with the gentle contrapuntal opening, symbolizing the promise of peace on Earth, portended by the birth of Christ. The evolution from the contrapuntal consonance of the opening into the brutal chromaticism symbolizing the chaos of war is brilliantly conceived, as is the emergence of hope that the message of the birth is taking hold. The glorious climax on a D major chord, preceded by impassioned outcries of "Friede auf der Erde"—Peace on Earth—is simply overwhelming! The outer edges of the work's chromaticism make it very challenging to perform. Its expressive intensity needs an opulent choral sound. Yet, if the sound is too rich, it makes it difficult to hear the chromatic complexity of the texture. The balance between textural clarity and expressive intensity is difficult to achieve. In Eric Ericson's[6] landmark recording, *Five Centuries of Choral Music*, he opts for a more crystalline clarity. For me, however, that tends to diminish the expressive power of the work.

Though I love the classical objectivity, the economy of means, and the structural clarity of Stravinsky, and I believe the *Symphony of Psalms* is, perhaps, the greatest choral work of the twentieth century, I find the powerful crying out for peace of "Friede" to be even more gripping. I am more of a Romantic creature; Schoenberg's chromaticism—extreme, brilliantly conceived, powerfully evocative, and so rich—presents an amazing journey to go through.

NOTES

1. Flummerfelt refers here to Barber's *Three Songs*, op. 45 (1974), premiered April 30, 1974 at Alice Tully Hall with renowned German baritone Dietrich Fischer-Dieskau (b. 1925, Berlin) singing and Charles Wadsworth accompanying.

2. The revised version was given its premiere by the Juilliard American Opera Center in 1975, and the Spoleto performances were presented at the 1983 festivals.

3. English poet Christopher Smart, 1722 (Shipbourne, Kent) to 1771 (King's Bench), spent his adult life in Cambridge and London, struggling with debt. He developed a religious mania and spent most of the time from 1756 to 1763 in institutions. *Jubilate Agno* was written in an asylum; it survives in fragments that were published as a definitive edition only in 1954 (from which Britten drew the poems for *Rejoice in the Lamb*).

4. British poet Wilfred Owen, 1893 (Oswestry) to 1918 (Ors, France), was twenty-five when he was killed in action, seven days before the Armistice of November 11, 1918. In 1917 he spent several weeks at the brutal French front, was injured and sent back to England. There, while convalescing, he wrote his best and most dramatic poetry, reflecting his horror at the atrocities of war—and our inability to stop them—with great pity and sorrow for his fellow soldiers.

5. The 1993 concert at Riverside Church in Manhattan, establishing the Dietrich Bonhöffer Chair in Theology and Ethics at Union Seminary and celebrating the life of this modern martyr, attracted musical dignitaries from around the world, including Flummerfelt and the Choral Artists, and conductor Christoph von Dohnányi, Bonhöffer's nephew.

6. Eric Ericson, b. 1918 (Borås, Sweden), conducted the Orphei Drängar of Uppsala University and was choirmaster of the renowned and oft-recorded Swedish Radio Choir, which he formed in 1951. He is an innovative teacher and champion of new music.

12

MESSIAEN

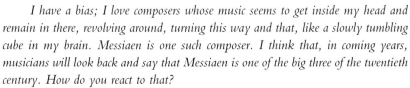

I have a bias; I love composers whose music seems to get inside my head and remain in there, revolving around, turning this way and that, like a slowly tumbling cube in my brain. Messiaen is one such composer. I think that, in coming years, musicians will look back and say that Messiaen is one of the big three of the twentieth century. How do you react to that?

Well, while I understand what you mean, I have difficulty embracing that. Maybe it's simply my own lack of understanding. I've thought a lot about why some of Messiaen's music eludes me. For sure, his little motet, "O sacrum convivium," is a radiant reflection of his deep faith. His *Quartet for the End of Time* is certainly a masterpiece. Perhaps it's because his composing is so much about color and about big chunks of sonorities, and less about organic evolution. Concerning color—as you know for Messiaen there is a direct relationship between specific visual colors and the music he composes to evoke or express them. His block-like structure, in its essentially vertical, nonorganic approach to the line, brings up the whole question of our cultural relationship to the passage of time.

How shall I say this? As time becomes ever more compressed—sped up, compacted—our perception of time as a linear phenomenon, as a thing moving forward in an evolutionary manner, gets skewed. I think that is, to a certain extent, what has given rise to the works of minimalist composers—music that is nonlinear, in the sense that it has no evolutionary aspect, no organic aspect. To me, that doesn't make any aesthetic or natural sense; however much our perception of time may be skewed, life is still an organic process. Again: the sun rises and it sets, we are born and we die, the tides

ebb and they flow, we breathe in and we breathe out. There is the ongoing tension/relaxation that is simply intrinsic to all of nature. In the case
of Messiaen, who is certainly no minimalist, the block-like nature of some
of his textures and the melodic and harmonic fragmentation of others lack
the aforementioned balance. Maybe that, in fact, makes him more in tune
with the age, and you may well be right about his musical stature in the
twentieth century.

In the Trois Liturgies, *the exact repetition of large "blocks" of music creates
for the listener a kind of trance, which is probably the point, like in* Turangalîla.
Yes, the passage of time feels suspended.

Talk a bit about Messiaen's interest in Eastern musical practices.
As a young organ student at DePauw I struggled to play some of his
early organ works and was bothered by what seemed to me to be a certain
lack of long, musical line. I think this was, in part, because of the way in
which Indian *ragas* influenced his rhythmic vocabulary. In his instrumental
works, his use of multiple gongs of Balinese origin is another example of
Eastern influences on his music. I have often thought that the next great
composer may be someone in whom there is a real amalgam or conver-
gence of things Eastern with things Western, which brings me back to the
whole vertical/horizontal question. One could say that Western culture has
been more horizontal, and the Eastern more vertical. That explains a lot
about how these two worlds have evolved historically. But, as our world
becomes more global, it is my fantasy that the next great musical voice will
be one in which the two cultural forces have perfectly coalesced, hence, a
kind of cultural nexus. Maybe Messiaen already got there.

He was also fascinated with bird calls.
He certainly was. That brings to mind a funny story. During my first
year at Westminster, the Symphonic Choir performed and recorded the
U.S. premiere of his major choral work, *The Transfiguration of Our Lord
Jesus Christ* with Antal Doráti[1] and the National Symphony in Washington.
Scattered throughout the piece are some seventy-odd birdcalls—that is,
musical passages played by a variety of instruments, each labeled as the call
of a particular bird. A year or two later, Pierre Boulez, then music director

National Symphony Orchestra

ANTAL DORATI, *Music Director*

FORTY-FIRST SEASON 1971-72

Tuesday Evening, March 28, 1972, at 8:30
Wednesday Evening, March 29, 1972, at 8:30
Thursday Evening, March 30, 1972, at 8:30

ANTAL DORATI, *Conductor*
YVONNE LORIOD, *Piano*
JANOS STARKER, *Cello*
WALLACE MANN, *Flute*
LOREN KITT, *Clarinet*
FRANK ANTHONY AMES, *Marimba*
JOHN A. C. KANE, *Xylorimba*
RONALD BARNETT, *Vibraphone*
WESTMINSTER SYMPHONIC CHOIR
  Joseph Flummerfelt, *Director*
  Michael Sylvester, *Tenor Solo*
  Paul Aquino, *Baritone Solo*

MESSIAEN   La Transfiguration de Notre Seigneur Jésus-Christ*

FIRST SEPTENARY

I. Gospel Narrative

Assumpsit Jesus Petrum, et Jacobum, et Joannem fratrem ejus, et duxit illos in montem excelsum seorsum: et transfiguratus est ante eos. Et resplenduit facies ejus sicut sol: vestimenta autem ejus facta sunt alba sicut nix.

Jesus taketh Peter, James, and John his brother, and bringeth them up into an high mountain apart, and was transfigured before them: and his face did shine as the sun, and his raiment was white as the light.

(St. Matthew, ch. 17, v. 1, 2.)

II. Configuratum corpori claritatis suae

Salvatorem exspectamus Dominum nostrum Jesum Christum, qui reformabit corpus humilitatis nostrae configuratum corpori claritatis suae.

We look for the Saviour, the Lord Jesus Christ, who shall change our vile body, that it may be fashioned like unto his glorious body.

(Philippians, ch. 3, v. 20, 21.)

Candor est lucis aeternae, speculum sine macula, et imago bonitatis illius. Alleluia.

For she [wisdom] is the brightness of the everlasting light, the unspotted mirror of the power of God, and the image of his goodness.

(Wisdom of Solomon, ch. 7, v. 26.)

III. Christus Jesus, splendor Patris

Illuxerunt coruscationes tuae orbi terrae: commota est, et contremuit terra.

The lightnings lighted the world: the earth trembled and shook.

(Psalm 77, v. 18.)

Christus Jesus, splendor Patris, et figura substantiae ejus.

Christ Jesus, the brightness of his Father's glory, and the express image of his person.

(Hebrews, ch. 1, v. 3.)

IV. Gospel narrative

Et ecce apparuerunt illis Moyses et Elias cum eo loquentes. Respondens autem Petrus, dixit ad Jesum: Domine, bonum est nos hic esse: si vis, faciamus hic tria tabernacula, tibi unum, Moysi unum, et Eliae unum.

And, behold, there appeared unto them Moses and Elias talking with him. Then answered Peter, and said unto Jesus, Lord, it is good for us to be here: if thou wilt, let us make here three tabernacles; one for thee, and one for Moses, and one for Elias.

(St. Matthew, ch. 17, v. 3, 4.)

A

Figure 12.1. Signed program of the U.S. premiere of Messiaen's major choral work, *The Transfiguration of Our Lord Jesus Christ*, with Antal Doráti and the National Symphony in Washington, D.C. A translation of Messiaen's note is "Thank you, dear Joseph Flummerfelt, for having given all your musicality and all your dynamism to this choir—who magnificently and religiously sang my work! Your true friend, Olivier Messiaen"

of the New York Philharmonic, was on our campus to rehearse, I don't remember what, for a Philharmonic performance. During the rehearsal we had a lunch break, and knowing that Boulez had been a student of Messiaen, I asked him if he could tell the difference between individual birdcalls. He kind of chuckled and said, "No."

Personally, Messiaen was a wonderful man—an almost saintly man, a man of deep faith. He was so dear when he came to the campus with Doráti to rehearse *The Transfiguration*. As you can imagine, many of the organ majors were Messiaen devotees, and those kids were sitting in the foyer of the Chapel clutching bouquets for him when he walked in. He took the flowers and responded in such a kind way. Needless to say, the students were enchanted.

The rehearsal began with Doráti conducting in the chancel of the campus chapel with Messiaen sitting close by. After we had sung the chorale that closes part 1, and it was really going well, Messiaen said, "*Formidable!*" At that moment, I breathed a huge sigh of relief, since, obviously, I was very anxious and hoped that this great composer would be happy with what he heard. The performances and the recording, which went on to win the Grand Prix du Disque de le Président de la République, went very well and he added an inscription to the choir in the introduction to the printed edition, which appeared some months later. I was very touched. Messiaen possessed this massive intellect, yet was child-like and had such a kindly nature. Back at DePauw playing those organ works, how could I have imagined this experience?

NOTE

1. Hungarian conductor and composer Antal Doráti, 1906 (Hungary) to 1988 (Gerzesee, Switzerland), was music director of the Dallas Symphony, the National Symphony, the BBC Symphony, and the Royal Philharmonic.

13

GLASS, ADAMS, AND
WORLD PREMIERES

Minimalism has become a very broad and undefined musical style. In fact, there is a newer kind of minimalism that is even more stark than that of minimalism's founding fathers. This ultrafocused style—in composers like David Lang[1] and Pelle Gudmundsen-Holmgreen[2]—seems less self-conscious, perhaps liberated by limitations, but owes a certain debt to those who first experimented with the style. You know Philip Glass and John Adams. Tell us about them.

I once had an interesting conversation with Philip Glass in Charleston. We were sitting together at a lunch party, and he talked about his own educational journey.[3] As a student at Juilliard he felt he didn't get the grounding he needed in counterpoint and harmony, so he went to study with Boulanger. With her, he got the rigorous training in the fundamentals that he was looking for. Even though I don't relate to his music, I came away from that lunch saying to myself, "This is a very serious musician."

He told me, "We were, we are . . ."—and he was talking about the "we" as in the minimalists "we"—"We're reacting to what we thought was the excessive complication of many contemporary composers." Though he didn't say so, I assumed he was talking about composers such as Boulez, Stockhausen,[4] Milton Babbitt,[5] and others. While I understand that motivation, what results is, for me, overly simplistic. In my admittedly limited experience, the music of some minimalist composers consists of patterns repeating relentlessly, with occasional pitch changes, slight rhythmic changes, or shifting sonorities. The music that results becomes sort of hypnotizing, but it's not going anywhere, and it is harmonically very static.

———❦———

Shaw told me he was once in the middle of a piece by Glass in Atlanta and the principal clarinet gave him a "What measure are we on?" shrug. He said, "I didn't know, I was just doing my best to keep it going. Then it comes to an end, and the audience leaps to its feet, yelling. And, I don't get it." So, why does the audience get it? What are they getting?

I wish I knew. One year, there was a Spoleto benefit concert for Charleston at Alice Tully Hall soon after Hurricane Hugo.[6] Many artists who had been part of Spoleto performed. Martha Graham's dancers, members of the Lincoln Center Chamber Music Society, Jean-Yves Thibaudet and many others were a part of that evening. Glass played a small piano piece for the occasion. Having just heard a succession of so many wonderful performances, I thought, "This just sounds like somebody noodling in C major. This is embarrassing." But the audience loved it! Like Shaw, I just don't get it.

It was clear from my conversation with Glass that he is a very serious musician who is not trying to fool anybody; this is just what he believes. But, I just don't get his music. What's it about? And you're right; how in the world do you conduct this when one can so easily get lost? I remember Christopher Keene once talking about this, just like your Shaw story. He was conducting some piece, got lost, and he turned to the concertmaster and said, "Where are we?" And the concertmaster whispered, "I don't know; I thought you knew." So how do you keep track of that? I certainly couldn't.

Maybe a lot of it is hype. I think there are folks who don't know what they think, but the press thinks it's really important, so they do too. It may be a lot about marketing. You can't convince me that it's going to be around in a few more generations. And, again, maybe that makes me too much of a traditionalist, but I just don't get music that doesn't evolve in a relatively organic manner. Probably *they* would say it evolves. I would say, changing a note, a rhythm, every so often—that's changing but it's not evolving. It's not going anywhere, because it's not been anywhere. There's no tension because there's no release. Ernst Toch's little book, *The Shaping Forces of Music*, says that all form is essentially the balance between tension and relaxation.[7] But isn't that also a life principle, which I spoke about earlier? In minimalism, the relentless repetition of whatever musical patterns, only slightly altered, creates a feeling of persistent tension that doesn't allow any relaxation or any structural breath to occur. And if that is missing, then

I just don't get it, because it doesn't relate to that balance of tension and relaxation which is implicit in everything that is alive.

John Adams?

I had the privilege and pleasure of preparing the world premiere and first recording of his *On the Transmigration of Souls,* which the New York Philharmonic commissioned to commemorate the first anniversary of 9/11. This work clearly reflects Adams' integration of minimalist practices into a larger, more organic musical fabric. As we prepared the piece, the Choral Artists and I felt we were participating in the premiere of something very special.

The work combines the forces of large orchestra, large chorus, and children's chorus, with speakers placed all around the hall. At the beginning, one hears street noises, then a numb repetition of "missing, missing," then the orchestra begins. Throughout the work, one hears the names of persons killed in the horror, called out by different voices. The orchestral and choral forces evolve to a point of cataclysmic force, then gradually merge into an evocation of the departed souls' existence in a state of perfect serenity and stillness. The performance had a powerful effect on performers and audience alike and the piece went on to win the Pulitzer Prize; the recording was awarded three Grammys.

What other first performances have been important?

With Masur in New York, there was the world premiere of a piece of Thomas Adès in which the Symphonic Choir had a small role, but which I thought was very powerful.[8] That's a composer with an amazing voice—really significant. It was part of a series of millennium commissions by the Philharmonic. We also premiered a piece of Kaija Saariaho, which *USA Today* called one of the ten most important performances of the year.[9] More recently the New York Choral Artists gave the world premiere of Peter Lieberson's[10] *The World in Flower* with the Philharmonic. Other premieres? We did the American premiere of Lukas Foss's *American Cantata*; Bernstein conducted. Stephen Paulus's[11] *Voices of Light,* which I premiered with the Philharmonic. Other American premieres included the Messiaen *Transfiguration,* the Penderecki *Magnificat,* and an oratorio of Antal Doráti, *The Call.* At the composer's request I conducted the world premiere of Carlisle

Floyd's[12] *A Time to Dance* with the Westminster Choir and the San Antonio Symphony for an ACDA national convention. Many years ago, at one of the first national ACDA conventions, my DePauw University Choir joined with Weston Noble's[13] choir for the world premiere of Daniel Pinkham's[14] *The Lamentations of Jeremiah*, with the composer conducting. Every time I see Weston, we both comment that that performance was probably its first and its last.

A genre that I'll call spiritual minimalism: Pärt and Górecki. I think it is quite different than Glass's minimalism.

I've only performed two pieces of Pärt: *Magnificat* and *The Beatitudes*. Neither of these pieces especially moves me, but they do intrigue me. I can imagine that, in the right situation—a cathedral-like expanse, an ensemble perfectly in tune, the timing exactly right, the balances perfect—they could be quite moving, evoking hovering timelessness within a remarkable spatial dimension.

So is it vertical music?

It might be better to call it hovering music. It exists in the moment, suspended in space and in time, and, in that sense, one might call the progress of the line "vertical."[15] That, along with its harmonic clarity, and the absence of rhythmic or melodic embellishment, contributes to its haunting, mystical quality.

NOTES

1. David Lang, b. 1957 (Los Angeles), won the 2008 Pulitzer Prize for his composition *The Little Match Girl Passion*. His early music was informed by his studies with Hans Werne Henze, but has evolved into a unique, highly contained, emotional minimalism. He cofounded the renowned new-music ensemble Bang on a Can.

2. Danish composer Pelle Gudmundsen-Holmgreen, b. 1932 (Copenhagen), is not bound by style but has been primarily focused on a "new simplicity," as a reaction to the "new complexity" of the time. His music is full of paradoxes—at once pessimistic yet warm, carefully organized yet intimate.

3. *Hydrogen Jukebox,* a collaboration of Philip Glass and "Beat poet" Allen Ginsberg, was commissioned by Spoleto USA and the American Music Theater Festival

(Philadelphia) and premiered in Charleston, South Carolina in 1990. The title is borrowed from a line of Ginsberg's poem "Howl" (1956). Glass writes:

> Drawing upon Ginsberg's poetry, this music/theater piece is a portrait of America that covers the 50's, 60's, 70's and 80's, seen by the collaborators Glass, Ginsberg, and Sirlin. Its content ranges from highly personal poems of Ginsberg to his reflection on social issues: the anti-war movement, the sexual revolution, drugs, eastern philosophy, and environmental awareness. The six vocal parts represent six archetypal American characters—a waitress, a policeman, a businessman, a cheerleader, a priest, a mechanic. (www.philipglass.com/music/compositions/hydrogen_jukebox.php)

4. The music of Karlheinz Stockhausen, 1928 (Cologne) to 2007 (Kürten), spans all genres and many styles. Notable works include *Gruppen* for three orchestras, *Stimmung* for six vocalists, *Tierkreis*, and the opera cycle *Licht* (which requires a week to be performed in its entirety). He is known for his groundbreaking work in electronic music, spatialization, and serial composition.

5. *Three Compositions for Piano* (1947), by Milton Babbitt, b. 1916 (Philadelphia), is one of the earliest examples of total serialization in music—music in which all parameters have been predetermined. A longtime Princeton University faculty member, he was interested in electronic music and worked for RCA on an early synthesizer.

6. Hurricane Hugo hit Charleston on September 21, 1989, and damaged many of the city's historic houses, churches, and theatres, many of which house Spoleto USA performances each summer.

7. Austrian composer Ernst Toch, 1887 (Vienna) to 1964 (Los Angeles), fled Germany after one of his operas was withdrawn by the Nazis; he taught at UCLA from 1937, was thrice nominated for an Academy Award for film scores, and won the 1956 Pulitzer Prize. *The Shaping Forces in Music* (1948, reprinted by Dover, 1977) is based on lectures he gave at Harvard in 1944. Attempting to reconcile traditional music to modern styles, Toch employs musical examples exhaustively to illustrate how music must respond to psychological needs in the listener, and how these needs are met by various musical styles. Describing tension, he writes: "The drama, too, unfolds through the medium of time and uses the mechanism of logical and psychological consecution. Here a plot is created, developed, lifted from level to level by continuously added intrigues . . . until in the last (often short) act, the intricate threads disentangle and no superfluous wordiness hampers the precipitation to the end" (160).

8. British composer Thomas Adès, b. 1971 (London), found enormous success at a young age through his operas: *Powder Her Face, Asyla,* and *The Tempest.* Adès' *America, A Prophecy* was a 1999 commission from the New York Philharmonic to celebrate the end of the millennium. Writing in *USA Today*, critic David Patrick Stearns named it among the year's worst new works, "a nasty prediction of America's demise." (In the same year he listed Adès as having composed the best new work of the year, *Asyla*, written in 1997).

9. Finnish composer (and Paris resident) Saariaho, b. 1952 (Helsinki), first reached international recognition in the 1980s with a commission from the Kronos Quartet. Her operas *L'amour de loin* and *Adriana Mater*, both collaborations with Peter Sellars, have secured her international stature. Stearns' *USA Today* review of Saariaho's *Oltra Mar: Seven Preludes for the New Millennium* refers to her "luminous, otherworldly textures."

10. American composer Peter Lieberson, b. 1946 (New York City), wrote his orchestral song cycles *Rilke Songs* (1997–2001) and *Neruda Songs* (2005) for his wife Lorraine Hunt Lieberson; they have been performed by many of the great orchestras of America. His work is influenced by his extensive studies in Tibetan Buddhism and Shambhala Training.

11. Stephen Paulus, b. 1949 (Summit, New Jersey), has served as composer in residence for several major orchestras, including Minneapolis (the birthplace of the American Composer's Forum). His *Voices of Light* (based on texts of thirteenth-century women, for women's choir and orchestra, 2001) was commissioned by Westminster Choir College to celebrate Flummerfelt's thirtieth anniversary at Westminster and the seventy-fifth anniversary of the college; Flummerfelt conducted the world premiere with the New York Philharmonic at Avery Fisher Hall on April 12, 2001.

12. Carlisle Floyd, b. 1926 (Latta, South Carolina), began his career as a pianist, and in 1947 joined the piano faculty at Florida State University. He is best known as a composer of opera; his most famous works are *Susannah* (1955), *Of Mice and Men* (1969), and *Cold Sassy Tree* (2000).

13. Weston Noble, b. 1922 (Riceville, Iowa), had a fifty-seven-year career at Luther College in Iowa, directing the Concert Band and making the Nordic Choir one of the most elite college choirs in the United States.

14. Daniel Pinkham, 1923 (Lynn, Massachusetts) to 2006 (Natick, Massachusetts), studied composition with Walter Piston and Aaron Copland at Harvard and with Samuel Barber, Arthur Honegger, and Nadia Boulanger at Tanglewood. He was on the composition faculty of both Boston Conservatory and the New England Conservatory of Music.

15. The style for which Arvo Pärt is best known he calls *tintinnabuli* (from Latin: "little bells"). In his words:

> I have discovered that it is enough when a single note is beautifully played. This one note, or a silent beat, or a moment of silence, comforts me. I work with very few elements—with one voice, two voices. I build with primitive materials—with the triad, with one specific tonality. The three notes of a triad are like bells and that is why I call it *tintinnabulation*. The style is, thus, composing two simultaneous voices as one line—one voice moving stepwise from and to a central pitch, first up then down, and the other sounding the notes of the triad. (Quoted in Paul Hilliard, *Arvo Pärt*, Oxford University Press, 1997, 87)

14

TWELVE TONE, TONALITY, AND PENDERECKI

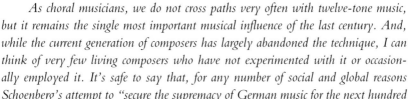

As choral musicians, we do not cross paths very often with twelve-tone music, but it remains the single most important musical influence of the last century. And, while the current generation of composers has largely abandoned the technique, I can think of very few living composers who have not experimented with it or occasionally employed it. It's safe to say that, for any number of social and global reasons Schoenberg's attempt to "secure the supremacy of German music for the next hundred years" failed, but there is no denying that the dominance of his discovery has lasted nearly that long. Where do you think twelve tone is right now?

Let's talk about the phenomenon of complexity in general, in terms of the three giants: Berg, Webern, and Schoenberg. I just don't relate to Webern's music. I've analyzed one or two of his cantatas. I recognize the craft, but his work just doesn't speak to me; it seems overly controlled. On the other hand, dodecaphony in the hands of Alban Berg is a whole other thing. *Lulu, Wozzeck,* the violin concerto, the *Lyric Suite*; these are all masterpieces. He made the twelve-tone technique work, but within the framework of classical form. Berg also has an extraordinary melodic gift. "De profundis" of Schoenberg is also a masterpiece.

Berg's music nearly always implies a tonal background— it's inherent even throughout his twelve-tone landscape, This is why Bernstein responded so easily to Berg—and not Schoenberg—because he believed tonality was in an "innate physical necessity."[1]

The whole issue of tonality, and the death thereof, is a real struggle for me, because, again, I'm so possessed with the idea that all art must have some roots in the natural. And clearly, common practice harmony is born out of the tension and release inherent in the overtone series. That is a natural phenomenon. If you take that away completely, what have you got? You mentioned Penderecki coming back to his more tonal self.

My reaction to what seems to be Penderecki's movement back to tonality may seem to contradict what I have just said. As I mentioned in my remarks about Shaw, I had an extraordinary introduction to his *St. Luke Passion* through our performances when I was quite young. Westminster Symphonic Choir later performed it with Doráti and the National Symphony. I thought then, and still do think, that the way Penderecki combines tone row-like neo-Palestrinian passages with sections using tone clusters, the interesting monody of the Evangelist, and passages with carefully notated rhythms along with aleatoric stretches all relate to the text in a very compelling way. I think it is an important work, and I am surprised that it seems to have disappeared from the repertoire.

Krzysztof himself conducted the Symphonic Choir and the Yale Symphony in the U.S. premiere of his *Magnificat* at Carnegie Hall and in New Haven. Both this work and his *Dies irae*, which we later performed with Mehta, are works of even greater complexity and reflect a composer who seemed very sure of his own voice.

After having worked with the *St. Luke Passion*, I found the *Magnificat* to be more challenging in certain ways. Part of the problem with early Penderecki is trying to get from the symbols to the sound, especially regarding temporal relationships. In the *St. Luke Passion*, I needed to add vertical, bar-like lines in order to reproduce temporally the spatial relationships on the page. Otto Mueller[2] was the Yale Symphony's conductor at the time and I remember him saying, "Krzysztof still has notational issues." In several places in the *Passion*, he indicated glissando lines and the singers were called on to calibrate the pace with which they moved through the pitches that the line crossed. Well, in the *Magnificat*, the earlier glissandi were replaced with lines moving in quartertones [see figure 14.1]. We worked and worked on these, and I knew we still weren't within gunshot of the exact pitches. And then, at Krzysztof's piano rehearsal with the choir in Princeton, we came to one of these horribly complex layers of multiple quartertone lines. We sang through it and he said, "No, no, no! Just go 'Ahhhhhhh'" and moaned in a big glissando sigh. Damn it! Why didn't he just draw some long gliss lines and everything would have been so much simpler!

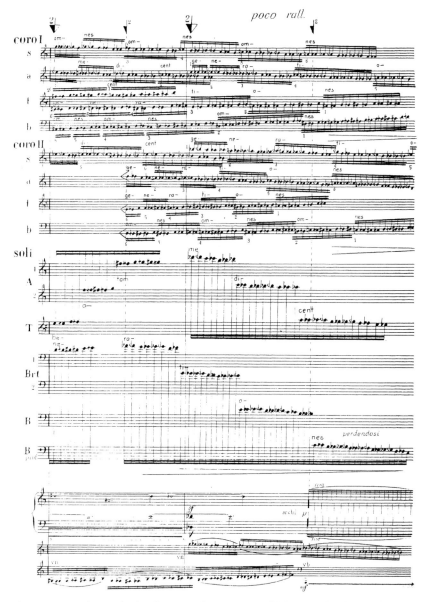

Figure 14.1.   The meticulously notated passage to which Joe refers in Penderecki's *Magnificat*, where the composer desires simply glissandi. © 1974 by SCHOTT MUSIC GmbH & Co. KG, Mainz, Germany. © Renewed, All Rights Reserved. Used by permission of European American Music Distributors LLC, sole U.S. and Canadian agent of Schott Music.

What about the St. Luke Passion?

Well it's interesting; when it was premiered in the sixties, some people considered it to be nearly as important as the *War Requiem*. I think it's fair to say it created that kind of stir. But, as I said earlier, it seems to have all but disappeared from the repertoire. Is it because it's very difficult?

It's very expensive to produce.

But so are a lot of other works. Maybe it just didn't have staying power. It has some very evocative moments, but I'm not sure it works as a whole piece. Some of the a cappella sections based on tone rows are quite beautiful. But there are other moments that, for me, just don't work, like certain passages of choral speech. It is a work of a fertile musical imagination, and it is a work of integrity. I wouldn't necessarily call it a work of genius.

Speaking of the *St. Luke* brings to mind a certain incident. As I said, I first prepared the FSU Singers for Shaw and the Atlanta Symphony in 1971. One day, during our final rehearsals in Atlanta, Shaw asked, "Do you know "The Old Rugged Cross"? Can you play it?" I said, "Sure, in any key." "Well," he says, "I'm going to give a lecture on the *Passion* for the Women's Guild of the Symphony and I want us to sing it for the ladies"—Atlanta patrons of the orchestra. At a certain point in his talk, he said, "Now Mr. Flummerfelt and I are going to sing for you." So, we sang "The Old Rugged Cross." I think I sang the tune and he sang the harmony in thirds. Then, he played a recording of the end of part 1 of the *Passion* where the crowd screams "Crucifige illum!" (Crucify him!). And then he says, "Now, tell me ladies, which one has more to do with a body suffering on the cross?" What a vivid way to help these ladies begin to understand how evocative this strange (to them) musical language could be.

With his *Requiem*, Penderecki has returned to a more conservative, quasi-tonal approach to composition.

It reflects—or perhaps, in view of his international stature, permits—the trend toward simpler building materials in composition. He says the age of experimentalism is coming to a close; yet, this evolution is very personal for him. It's not a matter of the age we're in. Rather, it is a matter of him getting in touch with his own need to express, and with his own humanity.[3]

So that begs the question: Is the *St. Luke Passion* somehow less human in his eyes?

Good question. I believe he would answer that those were the necessary expressions of the time because the age was one of experimentation.

But does that make it an arbitrary decision on his part, or was that his voice? Did he decide to use all those avant-garde techniques because it was au courant, or because that is who Krzysztof Penderecki was at that point? I think it's the latter.

His reasoning was exactly what you are talking about: it's a fundamental humanness, a tension and release, Western culture, the tension/release implied in the overtone series.[4] Did we return because we went to the edge of the cliff, and we just realized there was . . .

. . . nothing but a precipice down there? It's a good question, Donald, and, who knows the answer? Composers clearly have been working in a multitude of musical styles, searching for a voice, and though some interesting music has been and is being written, can one say that any one composer has emerged whom history will consider in the company of early twentieth-century giants such as Stravinsky, Bartók, Berg, and Britten? But then the world has become so complex that perhaps it is impossible for any composer to fully encompass the age. And that's why I came to my hypothesis about this coalescing of the East and West, and how that would manifest itself in the next Stravinsky, or the next Bartók, or the next Schoenberg, or the next giant—someone who synthesizes the two. Maybe, as I said earlier, Messiaen is such a composer.

Ton de Leeuw[5] tried, I believe, and Jonathan Harvey's[6] music sometimes also looks East. But, what about other people today—Corigliano,[7] Paulus—who write in clearly tonal, nonexperimental voices.

I've only performed Corigliano's *Fern Hill*, which was clearly influenced by Barber. As I've mentioned, Westminster commissioned Paulus's *Voices of Light* for Symphonic Choir and the New York Philharmonic. To be sure, Stephen's musical language is more conservative, but he is a man of great integrity, and for me, his love of text, and his ear for orchestral color—especially his use of percussion—is very interesting. Both these men have certainly not chosen their musical vocabulary in an arbitrary manner. Their musical language is simply what they hear.

———— ❦ ————

With vocal music, and therefore texted music, this tonal resurgence may reflect the influence of pop music; indeed, pop musicians have crossed over. Your foray into this has been with Paul McCartney.

The Choral Artists performed his oratorio *Standing Stone* in New York some years ago. When they called us to see if we were available, I agreed, though with some real reservation. McCartney is a very sweet and very sincere guy, who is not trying to hoodwink anybody. But he clearly has no musical skill in this genre—no craft at all. And he wrote things, which occasionally have some interesting colors and ideas, by just fiddling around on whatever kind of synthesizer he had or just by singing it. Somebody else wrote it down and Richard Rodney Bennett[8] orchestrated it. What resulted is incredibly derivative. We put it together in a short time, as it is really simple stuff, but I can't imagine how much it cost—for sure an enormous sum. Finally, it came across as a big indulgence, but the Choral Artists enjoyed it, no doubt because it was Paul McCartney.

NOTES

1. Bernstein's Charles Eliot Norton lectures at Harvard (autumn 1973) were collected and televised as *The Unanswered Question: Six Talks at Harvard* (Harvard University Press, 1976). In them he calls tonality "the poetry of the earth." At the time they were criticized for their level of detail, focus on tonal music and the direction that music was taking, and the unusual amount of interdisciplinary references—all things that, today, have come to be fashionable.

2. German conductor Otto-Werner Mueller, b. 1926 (Bensheim), was music director of the Victoria (Canada) Symphony Orchestra and has taught at the University of Wisconsin, Yale, Juilliard, and the Curtis Institute. He is a frequent guest of major symphony orchestras.

3. "Anyone who feels inclined to call my symphonies further instances of 'cathedrals of uselessness' should know that I freed myself a long time ago of the temptation of saving the world. I am far more concerned with saving what is most important for me in the artistic and human dimension." Krzysztof Penderecki, *Labyrinth of Time: Five Addresses for the End of the Millennium* (Hinshaw Music, 1998), 61.

4. In his book *Healing the Rift* (Continuum International, 2003), Ivan Hewitt addresses the current tonality: "Desire is indeed the engine of the new tonality. . . . Composers want that ready link with expressivity, and the connection with the

desire is often mixed with other things—resentment, or a determination to show that, though one wants the power of tonality, one isn't going to be bound by its protocols" (223).

5. Dutch composer Ton de Leeuw, 1926 (Rotterdam) to 1996 (Paris), was a student of Messiaen. His experiments with microtonality were influenced by time spent in India and his interest in "transculturation" was also informed by time in Japan. He was a longtime and influential teacher at the Sweelinck Conservatory in Amsterdam.

6. British composer Jonathan Harvey, b. 1939 (Sutton Coldfield), a student of Milton Babbit, was highly influenced by Karlheinz Stockhausen, then Pierre Boulez at IRCAM, where he wrote *Bhakti* (1982), recognized as an important work of its time. Based on texts of the *Rig Veda, Bhakti* brings together serial and electroacoustic techniques. He often employs chants and multidimensional layers and his music is informed by Buddhism.

7. John Corigliano, b. 1938 (New York City), became an international sensation with the December 1991 premiere of his opera *The Ghosts of Versailles* at the Metropolitan Opera. He won the 2001 Pulitzer Prize for his Symphony no. 2.

8. Richard Rodney Bennett, b. 1936 (Broadstairs, Kent), best known for film scores—*Murder on the Orient Express* (1974) and *Four Weddings and a Funeral* (1994)—has equal facility in jazz and classical idioms and performs as a jazz vocalist and pianist. He studied with Boulez and initially composed in a Neo-Romantic serialistic style; since the 1980s, he has written predominantly tonal music.

V

CHORAL SOUND, CONDUCTING,
AND CULTURE

15

WESTMINSTER CHOIR COLLEGE, VOICE BUILDING, AND CHORAL SOUND

My first semester at Westminster Choir College, you were on sabbatical and so I observed Frauke Haasemann[1] often, warming up the choirs and conducting rehearsals. I found all that barking like a dog and picking cherries with our lips a bit perplexing, if not comical, but eventually came to realize not only the technical worth of her group exercises, but also the community worth as well. You've often mentioned the influence that she had on you and on the Westminster choirs. Did that influence, of sound and voice building, remain in the choir after she died?

Frauke had a much larger influence on me than I realized at the time. I'm not sure I could even articulate it: an awareness of sound, or a "way of listening." I think I came to "sound" not insignificantly through the influence of being at Westminster. I brought with me a very different sound, one that didn't completely fulfill what I wanted to hear on the inside. When I got there, Westminster was a lot about sound, a sound that tended to be overlaid on every style period. I was influenced by Frauke—less in the *specifics* of her techniques and her famed voice building, and more by watching her warm up the choir and hearing what happened, especially in preparing a sound appropriate to the piece we were about to rehearse. But finally, much of what I learned from Frauke was by a kind of osmosis, which, as I've said, is the way in which I think a lot of essential learning happens.

The other thing—and, this is very important, though not related to Frauke as a voice builder—was her affirmation of me after she came. My situation with President Ray Robinson[2] was still tenuous; he still had some doubts about my value to the institution. And Frauke literally went to him and said some very affirming things about my musicianship and my importance to the college. That was very important to me, what with her coming from such a different musical background, and from a very close relationship with Wilhelm Ehmann[3]—and reacting so powerfully to what I did. As you can imagine, this meant the world to me.

On my first sabbatical, she arranged all kinds of important experiences in Europe. Many musical doors opened because of her. She was so connected to European choral life, and she knew so many conductors. Through her I was able to spend time with Eric Ericson, Helmuth Rilling,[4] Nikolaus Harnoncourt,[5] and many others. She let me use her house in Herford, Germany as my base. That's also where Ehmann's school was located. So, because of Frauke, that 1978 sabbatical in Europe was a significant learning time for me. In so many ways, Frauke's influence on my musical journey was beyond measure.

Frauke's influence on voice building through the choral experience was also huge throughout the United States. Through her many workshops, both at Westminster and around the country, she helped countless choral conductors learn how to work with sound more effectively. The impact of her influence was such that, following her death, the American Choral Directors Association dedicated its national convention to her.

Her voice-building ideas are largely designed for amateur choirs. Have you ever applied them to professionals?

No. Though it wouldn't be a bad idea, if the pros would respond to it. I wish I would feel comfortable starting—not vocalizing per se, not "voice building" but at least doing warm-ups to create ensemble and a sense of deeper listening.

Frankly, that's what I did with the Westminster Choir. By the time the kids got to me at the end of the day, they had already sung; they were all warmed up. On tour, the process began with the singers warming themselves up. Then, on the risers, we would always do vocalises designed to influence the line and listening. And, if I didn't do that, either on the campus or on tour—sometimes I wouldn't for whatever reason, maybe I felt pressed for time—I could tell. It always took us longer to get into a musical, ensemble mode. But I have to say, the whole business about warming up the choir? I didn't really know much about it until Frauke came along, because I came to choral music as a keyboardist, not as a singer. I had had several years of voice lessons in college, and had also learned from experiencing the warm-ups of Harold Decker and Elaine Brown, both of whom were singers. In more recent years, I've gone on to experiment, trying out new things. But having Frauke at my side for all those years was an incredible blessing, and it certainly embedded the importance of warm-ups and a much deeper vocal understanding in my approach to the choral art.

What stops you from doing it with the pros?
They would resist it. Of course, I'm always calling attention to matters of tuning, rhythm, articulation, balance, etc. But I am usually able to evoke ensemble through working on the music. The sound can be disparate in the beginning, but after a little work together, it starts to sound like an ensemble in a relatively short time.

Shaw used to say that professionals couldn't do what amateurs can.[6]
I believe that, in an ideal world, if you have the right group of professionals, with the right conductor, with all the time together that you do with amateurs, they should be better. They would bring to it much more life experience, vocal training, and musicianship. But, it is simply true that the economics of the profession don't allow that. In New York, for example, the Choral Artists, like all professional choirs in the city, is put together for a particular engagement, and doesn't have the luxury of the same group of singers regularly working and making music together. This is why conductors responded to the Westminster Choir so strongly. To be sure, the Choral Artists sing beautifully and have created many stunning performances. On the other hand, at Westminster the students live together, and work together almost daily, and everybody, or most everybody, loves what they are doing—the root of the word amateur, of course! They bring compassion and commitment. A performance is never a "gig," but an all-engrossing experience. Some professionals can be afflicted by a gig mentality and that just kills the impulse to go deep. But, again, I do believe that when such folks encounter the right musical leadership, and enough time together to remember why they went into music in the first place, they should be better. Don't you think so?

I don't think I've yet met a professional choral singer who didn't truly want the ensemble to be great and have meaning. I've seen it proven over and over again.

But, it only takes a few meaningless gigs for them to turn off and stop giving—to stop trusting—and the road back is often long and one of resistance.

Absolutely. The earlier Shaw Chorale sang with great passion and great love on recordings and on tour. Maybe you can say there was still a flicker of amateurism, because the whole American choral profession was just getting going. Shaw got it going. Maybe that's partially why Robert said pros can't do what amateurs can.

The whole sense of choral sound has changed in the last fifty years. I find it fascinating to hear the sound of Westminster Choir's Brahms Requiem recording under John Finley Williamson[7] and Bruno Walter, just before you came. The sound is incredibly different than with your choirs.

In the Bruno Walter recording, the old Westminster sound was very much the result of one man's concept of choral tone. It was Williamson's approach to vocal production; everything came with that sound. I was given the mandate to bring the Westminster choirs into the choral mainstream. Ken Jennings had that role with the St. Olaf Choir, which Anton Armstrong has continued.[8] Increasingly, stylistic awareness has caused all of us to become more attuned to, not only how choral sound needs to change between musical styles, but also how, even within works of one style period—especially those of the nineteenth and twentieth centuries—every composer calls for a different sound. Brahms doesn't sound like Verdi, who doesn't sound like Fauré; Barber doesn't sounds like Stravinsky, and so forth.

With respect to Williamson, it may also be that at a certain point, especially after the war, he had older students, particularly men. But certainly, also in his later years, he sought a very dark sound, and some people who sang with him told me that he emphasized a depressed larynx and high chest breathing.

So your first year at Westminster, were you up against that sound?

Yes. Not as entrenched as Williamson's, but yes, it was still there. Williamson was, I am told, an enormously charismatic man, though not a strong musician. He elicited a level of devotion from some of his students bordering on discipleship. Although he had retired in 1958, and I didn't arrive until 1971, his tonal approach was still very much in evidence because some of his voice teachers were still on the campus, and the leadership of the choirs in those intervening years had been mostly students of Williamson or graduates of the college.

You mentioned that Williamson was not a terribly strong musician.

This I heard from some of my colleagues—especially those on the organ faculty who had sung with him as students. My only firsthand experience of this happened when, after being in retirement for about four years, Williamson came back for the 1962 Westminster alumni week.[9] At that time I was in Philadelphia working with Elaine Brown, and one day she said, "You ought to go watch this." So, I took the train to Princeton and found a place in the balcony of Bristol Chapel, which was filled with alumni, all on the edge of their seats. It was a reading of the Brahms *Requiem* with Alexander McCurdy[10] at the organ. Williamson made this sort of gestural shudder, and the sound started—I wasn't quite sure how it happened. After a while I began to suspect that Williamson didn't really *know* the piece, and that McCurdy was leading from the organ! Many years later, some of my Westminster colleagues who were singing that day told me that my observation was not unfounded. I also learned that Williamson had others like Warren Martin,[11] a superb musician, train the choir, then he would come in and add the tone. And that tone was *dark*—apparently even too dark for Bruno Walter, who loved the choir. There are stories of Walter trying to coax some brighter German vowels out of them, to get "Selig" instead of "Sughlugh."

At some point, I considered Westminster for my master's degree. I visited the campus in the spring of 1958, because I wanted to study with Julius Herford, who was then on the faculty. I went to the Playhouse and watched the choir rehearse. Someone else was doing the rehearsal, but I just couldn't accept the sound or the tuning. Then I spoke with Mrs. Williamson,[12] who was dean, and just didn't relate to her. So, I didn't go there. How interesting, considering what subsequently evolved.

So, as you can imagine, when I first went to Westminster, I was a real outsider and ran into a lot of resistance. People didn't understand my language; they didn't understand my attempt to evolve a sound that was relevant to the piece we were doing. But I must admit, that, at that point, I was also not able to address these issues in a more helpful and less threatening way.

———⟨⟨⟨———

In addition to Frauke, who were your closest collaborators at Westminster and what did they bring to the equation?

Along with her, three people were at my side in the work of the choirs, and each of them made an enormous contribution to the work that resulted.

You earlier mentioned our dear friend Glenn Parker, now no longer with us. His artistry, his huge intelligence, and his keyboard brilliance were a constant source of musical wisdom and inspiration during the years he accompanied the Westminster Choir. So often I turned to him for insight and, as you well know, his skill with languages was unsurpassed. Also, in his role as a vocal coach and director of the opera program, Glenn had an enormous influence on the musical growth of our students. A number of them have gone on to major careers, and, to a person, they always cite Glenn as the finest coach-accompanist they ever worked with.

After Glenn I had the great good fortune to have Nancianne Parrella, another wonderful musician, at the keyboard for both Symphonic Choir and Westminster Choir. Nanci is a choral accompanist of rare skill. With her fabulous ears she always knew just what to do to help the rehearsal progress. Her amazing ear for intonation, balance, and her wonderful sense of tempo relationships were always an invaluable source of insight and greatly influenced the work of both choirs. As the associate director of the choir, she was of great help, both with sectionals and the occasional full rehearsal. Because she is such a warm and caring being, singers would often come to her with this or that concern, which she always responded to in the most helpful way. Both Nanci and her husband Joe remain among my dearest friends.

After Frauke, my very gifted colleague Andrew Megill was the associate conductor of the Westminster Symphonic Choir. He did all the warm-ups, as well as sectionals and full rehearsals as needed. His insightful response to what took place in rehearsals was invaluable. His knowledge of choral repertoire is legendary and I often turned to him for help in building a program for the Westminster Choir. For sixteen years Andrew was totally responsible for preparing the Westminster Choir for its work in the operas at the Charleston Spoleto festival. They were always beautifully prepared.

I could go on and on about other colleagues who meant so much to me and to the work of the choirs. One of the blessings of being at Westminster Choir College is its great voice faculty, nearly all of whom support and value the choral focus of the college. I needn't tell you how rare that is in most schools of music.

When Westminster was considering merging with Rider University, there was a groundswell of resistance from alumni fearing that Westminster would lose its identity, its charm, and the uniqueness of being a college where total enrollment seldom topped 300. Indeed, when I attended in the mid-eighties we hadn't yet entered the age of litigation and things were a bit loose around the edges. I am certain that for you and your colleagues who lived through the change, it had a significant impact on your work. So, post-merger, how has it changed?

Well, Westminster would not have survived if it hadn't affiliated with Rider. Some degree programs have evolved that would not have otherwise been possible, and the Rider connection also helped significantly increase Westminster's faculty salaries. In the first years it was not always easy because the cultures are so different, although support for the choral focus and mission of Westminster remained strong. The relationship has smoothed out, and a recent restructuring has allowed Westminster Choir College to evolve in a very productive way.

Has the nature of the students or the esprit de corps changed over the years?

I don't think so, except insofar as students have changed the world over. Westminster continues to get a full measure of very talented students, especially because of the world-class strength of the voice faculty, though fewer come with as rich a choral background, because not as many grow up singing in church choirs as was once the case. Also, the importance of choral music in high schools has, over the years, sadly, diminished.

When Westminster was free standing, there was a greater sense of family on the campus. Although, I believe a strong feeling of community still exists there. There is a lack of unhealthy competition; students support one another and the intrastudio competition that plagues many schools of music is not present. The philosophical core of the school is intact, and that's what has given it its essence—students come together nearly every day to make music. The community-building aspect of corporate music-making is a powerful binding force.

NOTES

1. German singer, conductor, and teacher Frauke Haasemann, 1922 (Rendburg, Schleswig-Holstein) to 1991 (Princeton), was particularly devoted to music of the

Baroque, performing and recording many Bach cantatas with Wilhelm Ehmann. She came to Westminster in 1977 to prepare the Westminster Choir for Ehmann's visit, then permanently joined the faculty to teach group vocal techniques. Her books include *Handbuch der chorischen Stimmbildung* (1984), *Voice Building for Choirs* (with Wilhelm Ehmann, 1981), and *Group Vocal Technique* (1990).

2. Ray Robinson was president of Westminster Choir College from 1969 to 1987, an artistically fertile though financially challenging time. (The finances improved when Westminster merged with Rider College—now University—in 1988.) Robinson is the author of numerous books, including several about Krzysztof Penderecki.

3. German conductor Wilhelm Ehmann, 1904 (Freistatt) to 1989 (Freiburg-in-Breisgau), formed the Evangelischen Kirchenmusikakademie in Herford in 1948; it remains the most important church music institute in Germany. A Bach and Schütz specialist, Ehmann taught Summer Sessions at Westminster and returned in 1978 to perform and record the Bach motets with the Westminster Choir. He is the author of *Choral Directing* (1968).

4. Helmuth Rilling, b. 1933 (Stuttgart), is best known for his performances and recordings conducting the works of Johann Sebastian Bach, often with his Stuttgart Bach Collegium and Gächinger Kantorei. He founded the Oregon Bach Festival which has commissioned a number of major works (including Penderecki's *Credo*, for which Rilling won a Grammy Award).

5. Austrian conductor Nikolaus Harnoncourt (Count Nikolaus de la Fontaine und d'Harnoncourt-Unverzagt), b. 1929 (Berlin), founded the Concentus Musicus Wien, one of the first period-instrument ensembles. He is a widely recorded conductor of historically informed performances of music through the early nineteenth century.

6. Shaw said, "When you get right down to it, to be an artist *is* to be an amateur. One can no more think of being a professional musician than he can of being a professional person" (letter to the Collegiate Chorale, 5 November 5, 1953).

7. John Finley Williamson, 1887 (Canton, Ohio) to 1964 (Princeton), founded the Westminster Choir School at Westminster Presbyterian Church of Dayton, Ohio in 1926. It soon moved the school to Ithaca, then settled in Princeton in 1932. Under Williamson's leadership, the Choir College established relationships with the Philadelphia Orchestra and New York Philharmonic that continue today. He was the president of the college until 1958.

8. Kenneth Jennings, b. 1925, earned his doctorate at the University of Illinois. He was the third conductor of the famed St. Olaf Choir, succeeding Olaf C. Christiansen, who succeeded his father F. Melius Christiansen; the latter formed the choir in 1912 and conducted it until 1943. Jennings was succeeded in 1990 by Anton Armstrong whose doctoral dissertation at the University of Michigan was about the evolution of the St. Olaf Choir.

9. Charles Schisler's doctoral dissertation, *A History of Westminster Choir College, 1926–1973* (1976, Indiana University), traces in detail, through interviews and

citations of the minutes of the Board of Trustees' meetings, the difficult circumstances surrounding the retirement of John Finley Williamson, president of the college, and his wife Rhea, who was dean. According to these sources, the Williamsons spoke of retirement in hope that the board—until then essentially reporting to Dr. Williamson—would not let them go. Conversely, the board took the opportunity to move in a new direction, feeling the time was overdue for change. Resentment formed in the Williamson camp, contributing to the difficult years to follow. Robert Shaw was offered the presidency, but declined. Dr. Ralston Smith, a minister in Oklahoma City, was also offered the position and declined. Dr. William F. MacCalmont, pastor at Westminster Presbyterian Church in Akron, Ohio, finally accepted the position, requiring that the Williamsons be banned from campus. MacCalmont came to face the challenge and necessity of accreditation and other internal problems that would not be solved until the subsequent administration of Lee Hastings Bristol, Jr., for whom Bristol Chapel, the on-campus house of worship and concertizing, is named.

10. Alexander McCurdy, 1905 (Eureka, California) to 1983 (Philadelphia), was head of the organ departments at the Curtis Institute of Music and Westminster Choir College. Also a conductor, he was a highly influential teacher and considered one of the world's great organists.

11. Warren Martin, 1916 (Galeton, Pennsylvania) to 1982 (Princeton), graduated from Westminster Choir College in 1936 and served on its faculty from 1952 until his death. For Westminster's commencement ceremony he composed *Processional for Organ* and *Anthem of Dedication,* for double chorus and organ, the latter taking advantage of the antiphonal seating arrangements—the underclassmen seated in the nave and the graduating class in the sanctuary.

12. Rhea Beatrice Parlette Williamson, 1888 (Dayton, Ohio) to 1967 (Scranton, Pennsylvania), met John Finley Williamson at Otterbein College in Ohio. She cofounded the Westminster Choir School and served as dean until retirement in 1958.

16

CONDUCTING

What makes a conductor great? Let's use Bernstein as a model; what did he exude that made him a great conductor?

Leonard Bernstein exuded a charisma, an aura, a kinetic energy that was unlike any other conductor I've worked with. With all of his flamboyance, with all of his—you know, what he was often criticized for—"histrionics," I really came to believe that his gestures were absolutely authentic, because they grew out of his powerful emotional attachment to music. That was why his Mahler was so great; he could go into that world—of Mahler's stream of consciousness—and live there. *And*, he was a consummate musician; he had great ears, he had a fabulous sense of rhythm, and a total grasp of the music's architecture. He projected this convulsive energy, yet he could also evoke a serene and tender long line. His capacity to make a long line work at a slower tempo was greater than anyone I've encountered, because of his intense inner rhythm. He was sometimes criticized because his gesture tended to subdivide most of the time; there was a sort of clicking going on. But it never intruded on the line.

With all of his huge gifts, Leonard Bernstein approached every score with great humility. Of all the conductors with whom I've worked, he had perhaps the most wide-ranging intellect. He was a genuine Renaissance man. His knowledge of philosophy, religion, literature, and the arts was astounding. And, of course, this contributed to the breadth and the depth of his music-making.

So what makes a conductor great? Obviously, musical mastery: great ears, a powerfully embodied sense of rhythm, the capacity to internalize complex scores, and a gestural vocabulary that vividly communicates musical ideas. Passion is critical, as is a theatrical flair. It is no accident that every major conductor has, at some time, worked in an opera house. In the case of Bernstein, although his career was largely symphonic, his few operatic performances were legendary.

A conductor needs to be deeply cultured and very intelligent. A great conductor must approach every musical masterwork with humility, yet also possess a very strong will that allows him or her to convey an absolute sense of certainty to the players or the singers. Finally, there is that elusive thing called charisma. And, a kind of communicative gift that is almost metaphysical and can't be verbalized.

You have many times prepared the same works for different conductors—sometimes more than once for the same conductor. It's part of what gives you such insight into both the works and the conductors. But, it begs this question: how do you pick up yet another Mozart Requiem *to prepare it for someone else?*

Because I love the work. It still feeds me.

Does it ever become mundane or routine?

No. If I didn't love the work, it would be dreary. It's never boring with Mozart's *Requiem*, or Beethoven's Ninth or any masterwork. Great music is an inexhaustible source. And, it's always a new experience with a different bunch of folks exploring a work. It's always fresh.

Talk about the difference between preparing and conducting. For example, you prepared the Brahms Requiem *for Masur several times, and now you've conducted it yourself several times. Is there a difference in preparing?*

I don't think so. Again, I prepare them as if I'm going to conduct them. Otherwise, I don't think it would work. There are certain characteristics of each conductor that one understands if one works with them regularly. For example, I knew that Masur's tempos sometimes tended to be on the fast side, so I might rehearse a piece faster than I would normally take it, just to alert the singers for that possibility. With respect to the specifics: I rarely sit down with a conductor—no one has the time—and I virtually never get a marked score, so I don't know what a conductor is going to ask for ahead of time. If the conductor has recorded a work, I will listen to it once to see if there are any surprising tempi, dynamics, etc. For example, with Masur: If it was a work he had recorded, like the *Missa solemnis*, I would listen to his recording, just so I was not way off base in respect to tempi, certain phrasing, etc. But, finally, I prepare it as if I were going to do the piece myself. Otherwise it doesn't come from an authentic place, and it's therefore not alive. It won't be flexible. If I were mechanically trying to impose what I think the conductor is going to do, it would have no organic quality; it would tend to be very stiff. That's why the transfer from my rehearsals to the conductor's piano rehearsal works easily. This is all due to gesture: since I communicate a lot gesturally, they respond to another conductor's gesture naturally.

One of the many things I've learned from you is to watch a conductor, hear what they say, then go back to the rehearsal room with the chorus and say "This is what they mean," and then help the chorus to achieve that.

Oh, I certainly do that, of course—interpret their musical ideas for the choir, yes—but that's in the final stages. But, we were talking about the beginning of the process. And in the beginning, I proceed as if I were going to conduct the performance. I don't know any other way to do it.

17

CULTURE

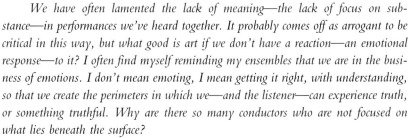

*We have often lamented the lack of meaning—the lack of focus on sub-
stance—in performances we've heard together. It probably comes off as arrogant to be
critical in this way, but what good is art if we don't have a reaction—an emotional
response—to it? I often find myself reminding my ensembles that we are in the business of emotions. I don't mean emoting, I mean getting it right, with understanding,
so that we create the perimeters in which we—and the listener—can experience truth,
or something truthful. Why are there so many conductors who are not focused on
what lies beneath the surface?*

Well, one answer may be that even in our finest schools of music, the
emphasis is too much about achieving technical proficiency and too little
about the meaning. Also, I think there is a tendency for the curriculum of
doctoral programs in choral conducting to be so focused on the research
side of music study that, again, music-making is approached from the outside in, instead of the inside out. I think our choral world is often overly
focused on matters of the tone, pitch, blend, appearance, etc., and too few
conductors talk about the thing that finally gives it life, what motivates the
musical gesture from the inside. So often we hear well-crafted performances
that leave us cold, because nothing magical is happening. Also in the orchestral field, there are conductors where the performances are too much
about them instead of about the composer.

Many people mistake surface for substance, which is a cultural affliction of our time that affects the education of musicians. Consider schools
of music, high-powered schools that turn out instrumentalists who play
with great virtuosity and great brilliance. And you say, "OK, it's kind of

impressive, but now what?" And singers? Good Lord! I call certain ones "sound machines": people with extraordinary voices—who pay thousands and thousands of dollars to develop their voices—but seem to stay focused on that sound and fail to connect with what motivates it musically. The result is singing that, however opulent the sound, is one-dimensional and lacks the vast, wonderful color range that makes the human voice so special. No one has led them to understand that *truth*, whether in music or in life, flows from the inside out, not the other way around.

Marcel Proust wrote: "Our vanity, our passions, our spirit of imitation, our abstract intelligence, our habits have long been at work, and it is the task of art to undo this work of theirs, making us travel back in the direction from which we have come, to the depths where what has really existed lies unknown within us."[1]

Absolutely true, which takes us back to the starting point: the thing that finally gives any vocal sound communicating power is the extent to which it is connected to the primal cry. That's the human core from which sound must emanate. It think we've arrived at our current affliction through our propensity to mistake the surface for the substance, to accept the surface as having substance, to accept form without content, to mistake the appearance for the reality of the thing. This results in part from our inability to be silent, to stand still, to seek solitude, to look, to listen, to breathe.

Always the breath! Why have we gone there?

Well, I think we've gone there because of the increasing power of technology over our lives—for example, the increasing speed and perception of time. You consider that time was first measured by the moon, and then by the sun, and then it was measured by some primitive clock that maybe counted the days. Then we got around to the hours, and now where are we? Nanoseconds. I don't know even what they are! So the horizontal has gotten so fast that one can't experience the vertical. The speed of life and the speed of communication—all these things which are, on one level, wonderful and miraculous, and have given birth to this information age —have robbed us of the capacity to be vertical—to slow down, to go deep. Here we are again: head and heart. When head and heart intersect, it creates a balance. Vertical time is heart time and horizontal time is head time. It is the reason we're in such a hell of a cultural pickle, because continually careening forward keeps us on the surface, where life is very one-dimensional. Descartes said, "I think, therefore I am." But Pascal said, "The heart has its reasons, which reason cannot know." Well, maybe culturally we're trapped in the Descartesian world. The brain, technology, to know but not to understand, also the increasing availability of—and appetite for—instant gratification, all certainly keep us from taking the time to go deep.

Proust again: "If we read the new masterpiece of a man of genius we are de-lighted to find in it those reflections of ours that we despise; joys and sorrows which we have repressed, a whole world of feeling we had scorned, and whose value the book in which we've discovered them suddenly teaches us."[2]

Again, that's exactly right, because of our propensity to blot out the dark side, to blot out the underside, to ignore that which is unsavory about ourselves—the dirty and gritty, the primitive, animal thrust—which we abhor, which we tamp down, which we try to cover over.[3] The ugliness within us, the dark, the unsavory, the undesirable, the imperfect. We're really uncomfortable with that. But we have to embrace it somehow; we have to embrace it to become whole, to balance the dark and the light, the yin and the yang. Without the dark, there is no light. The notion that one can only live in the light? Well, I don't think that's being fully alive. It disconnects from the primitive, it disconnects from that other darker world that is an essential part of the whole.

As a result of forty years of working with ensembles, what do you know about people?

I believe that people in general long for some deeper connection. I think, for example, that the whole drug culture is a manifestation, albeit totally misbegotten, of trying to get connected to a state of being that has been lost. With respect to music education, at whatever level, if we can lead our students to the voices of Brahms, Beethoven, Bach, Stravinsky, Bartók, whomever, they find a connection with a human/spiritual core that unknowingly they have avoided. I'm really sure people long for this connection. The world is desperate for connection, and yet often goes after it in all sorts of misbegotten ways. And this desire for connection is why I believe every person is intrinsically creative to some extent. As a teacher of conducting I have always tried to help my students get in touch with their own creative core. With respect to those who have sung with me, I nearly always talk about the music and try to lead them, both through my gesture and by what I say, to a deeper understanding of the musical work at hand. By opening myself through the breath, by making myself vulnerable, I hopefully allow them to risk being vulnerable and thus to reach their own creative impulse. For sure, I have strong feelings about how a given piece should go, but hopefully these feelings grow out of a connection with the composer's voice and not out of a need for self-aggrandizement.

Respond to this common statement: Most choral conductors have problems conducting orchestras.

True, sadly true, maybe because there are a number of them who aren't also instrumentalists. Or, it may be something as basic as learning to read a full score. I don't think it's intrinsic, however, because in Europe I believe that's not the case. In general, European choral conductors seem more comfortable in front of orchestras. But, in this country, it is certainly true; we are often looked upon as second-class citizens musically. And maybe it's because there are far too many who aren't complete musicians. The training of choral conductors, unlike orchestral conductors, frequently dwells far too much on so-called choral techniques instead of building musicianship through rigorous work in ear training, sight singing, developing rhythmic skill, and score analysis, resulting in conductors who have big gaps in basic musicianship.

Is that related to your pronouncement, "I hate choral music"?

Hah! Well, I say that a little for its shock value. What I mean is that a choral performance —however perfectly executed—that all sounds the same, that lacks a color range, that doesn't go deep, that is too much about presentation and too little about penetration, just doesn't interest me.

Our conversation keeps leading us back to cultural frustrations: lack of cultural education, more interest in the surface than the interior, vacuous virtuosity. Norman Lebrecht—author of The Maestro Myth *and* Who Killed Classical Music—*attributes the death of classical music in part to the first Three Tenors concert, televised internationally from the World Cup. He says the crisis in conducting is twofold: there is a dearth of fresh talent and an alarming superficiality in the state of symphonic interpretation.*

I don't entirely agree. To be sure, there are some who ask, "Where are the Furtwänglers, the Klemperers, the Bruno Walters, or even the Toscaninis today?"[4] Yet, there are great musicians such as Abbado, Muti, Barenboim, Haitink, Levine, Masur, and many others active in the field. It might be said that today's younger generation lacks the interpretive weight of older generations, yet they can handle complex contemporary music and music before Haydn and Mozart in a way that some of their elders could not.

Certainly, the Three Tenors concert was a lot about hype and entertainment, and not about deeply rooted cultural values. Yet all of them were great singers and Mehta is certainly a major conductor. I do think that the market-driven world is too much with us. In the case of conductors, this may result in someone of greater talent being overlooked, and someone less gifted emerging because he or she has caught the press's fancy. But I don't think you can finally foist a complete fraud off on the symphonic world. I don't think there's anybody in a position of significant orchestral authority, including the younger generation, who is not talented, or not very good at what they do. I think marketing becomes the greater villain in the world of popular culture and, for that matter, in the world of contemporary art.

The marketing machine discourages a cultural elite. What are your thoughts on this looming destruction of the cultural elite?

That's another question to which there is no real answer. It comes back to education. I absolutely believe—and it has been corroborated over and over—that when you lead people into something that has greater substance and greater human value, they stop settling for things that are phony or artificial or superficial. But, you have got to get them there. And, the way you get them there is to get them when they're young, in schools. And that's obviously not happening. So, I don't know what we are to do. It *is* very disturbing.

Perhaps because people are not educated in the role of "culture"—and to an understanding of the purpose of a cultural elite— culture itself is viewed negatively.

That's a populist mentality that I believe infects our world today. That's a whole other issue. Look at the leveling of students in education. But, aren't people beginning to finally wake up to the fact that this is all out of whack? By all means, let's give every human being every opportunity to evolve and to grow. Fine. But let's not pretend that everyone is equally gifted or equally intelligent. What really concerns me is that the more gifted students are not always sufficiently challenged.

I have enough belief in the fundamental nature of humankind that eventually the recognition and appreciation of quality will be able to conquer, or overcome, this embrace of mediocrity, because leveling in the middle is settling for the mediocrity that keeps those more gifted from developing their full potential. A populist view of culture in which there is no hierarchy of values, and everyone and everything gets swallowed up in a general leveling, is for me, democracy gone too far. And like every movement in history, things swing too far in one direction and eventually swing back to equilibrium. I sure hope so.

It's encouraging to hear you say that.

That optimism comes from my fundamental belief in the fact that truth will prevail—eventually—though that doesn't always seem evident.

NOTES

1. Alain de Botton, *How Proust Can Change Your Life* (Vintage International, 1998), 103.

2. de Botton, *Proust*, 29.

3. Jared Diamond describes this in *The Rise and Fall of the Third Chimpanzee* (Hyperion Perennial, 1993):

> That our urge to kill is restrained by our ethics almost all the time is obvious. The puzzle is: what unleashes it? Today, while we may divide the world's people into "us" and "them," we know that there are thousands of types of "them," all differing from each other as well as from us in language, appearance and habits. It is hard to transfer ourselves back into the frame of mind prevailing throughout much of human history. Like chimps, gorillas, and social carnivores, we lived in band territories. The known world was much smaller and simpler than it is today; there were only a few known types of "them," one's immediate neighbors. (297–98)

4. For example, Toscanini's musical lineage: he played cello in the La Scala pit for the premiere of Verdi's *Otello* in 1886 and knew its librettist, Arrigo Boito. He conducted more *Falstaffs* than any other opera. He worked so closely with Puccini on his final opera, *Turandot* (1924, unfinished), that he made many additions and revisions after the composer died.

VI

CONCLUSION

18

FINAL WORDS

Gabriel Garcia Marquez tells us in One Hundred Years of Solitude, *"The secret to a good old age is simply an honorable pact with solitude." You've often talked about your need for this—the need to be alone.*

It's really essential for me. I'm grateful that solitude and silence don't frighten me.

How does it work that a person so capable of solitude—and I say that as a person who only recently discovered its value—makes art in a medium that requires so many people?

I don't have an easy answer for that. Maybe it's simply because my response to the music, and my passion to share that, requires I completely open up in order to fully connect with singers. Therefore, it is because I must, of necessity, spend whatever human resources are needed to communicate in that context that I feel the need to find regeneration in the peace and quiet of solitude.

How does a conductor—surrounded by hundreds of people looking to connect with them off the podium as well—give the time without suffocating or being false?

To be sure, there are those times when you just want to say "Leave me alone!" But, if your life goal is to be ever more authentic, and ever more connected, and to increasingly embrace the sum total of who you are, then the center is always there. And, although you develop ways of protecting yourself, you don't need the entourage; you don't need the protectors. You will, by virtue of who you are, create whatever insulation you need, when you need it. Also, you can step off that podium, and you can talk to somebody for a brief moment, and make some kind of a connection with him or her, because you're OK within yourself. Therefore it's authentic, and therefore they get something from it. You think of the great people you've encountered. Boulanger, for example, with all her unbelievable gifts; when she looked at you, when she talked to you, there was a connection.

When I am on the podium there is a connection to everything—everyone—around me. But there is also this feeling of solitude as I'm conducting—I suppose it's a kind of peace I have not yet been able to find outside of music-making. Do you share that experience?

I'm not certain I do—at least, not as solitude. As for a sense of being connected to everything, I do long for those moments where everything is in place, where everything is flowing, and then the truth comes from the source—whatever that is: God, the creative impulse, it doesn't matter what you call it. And suddenly, things happen, which you couldn't have planned. Real beauty is being created because all of the forces are perfectly lined up and a profound innermost connection is manifested. We then become a kind of conduit for an almost transcendental expressive force that could never emerge if we were simply, willfully trying to make it happen. I keep saying to my conducting students—stop thinking, let go, just listen. Then you have the possibility of a deep, intuitive connection to the music.

We always come back to sound: your ears start the sound, not your hands.
My ears, and the breath that initiates the sound.

In so many ways, you talk about the need to always be in the moment—to allow the unplanned thing to happen, to be spontaneous.

Yes. I remember when I was about twenty-four, when I was studying with Elaine Brown, I asked her, "When does the music one makes achieve a balance between perfection and spontaneity?" She smiled knowingly, and said, "Four, five times—very few times." And I accepted that then, but I don't accept that now. If you have built in the musical disciplines and have the courage to stop overcontrolling, and thus become able to listen deeply and to connect with your musical forces in a manner that allows a kind of creative circuitry to flow between conductor and performers, then glimmers of that ideal balance can emerge with some frequency. The perfection of the craft holds and spontaneity happens. And that brings me back to the breath. Out of that opening—out of that connection—comes the connection to a deeper source, which allows the truth to flow in and allows us to be really in the moment, which therefore, allows for something completely unplanned, completely spontaneous to emerge. This is why I have a problem with a lot of music-making today. It's about a technical perfection at the expense of "in-the-moment-ness," and spontaneity.

You mention "the source" and you allow the possibility even to equate that with God. It brings up a rather sensitive topic—one with which I certainly have struggled. Let's call it worship.

When you confront a B Minor Mass, a *Missa solemnis*, even a *Symphony of Psalms*, you are aware that the greatness of this work and the truth that lies beyond the confines of anyone's ego has to come from an eternal source. Bach was, surely, one of the greatest of all musical geniuses. What makes Bach great? What is the principal gift of Bach or Beethoven or Mozart? And my answer is "the gift of connection." Now, clearly there was a mastery of craft; that is essential. But what allows the music of a great composer to enrich our human understanding and to help quench our spiritual thirst is that, at the moment of creation, the composer was connected to a divine source, a powerful creative impulse. I call that source "God." Not God as prescribed by any religious beliefs, but the designation used as a symbol, albeit inadequate, of a creative power that motivates great works of art.

I do believe that we are created in the image and likeness of God. That God is within and without. In a very real sense, all I have been talking about is surrendering to, connecting with, breathing into that source within each of us. Therefore, I believe that every human being has some measure of this creative power. It's only that the giants have been given the gift of having it in far greater measure than you or me.

You know, I have this great interest in crafts, an interest in the things people make—like my Santa collection.[1] I knew this man in West Stockbridge, Massachusetts, for example. He retired and discovered he had a gift for carving. So, he created wonderful Santa Clauses in many guises. He wasn't a great artist, but he discovered he had a creative gift. I remember reading a story some years ago about women in some remote area in the South who create beautiful quilts. Maybe they're not artists; maybe they're simply artisans. Nonetheless, every human being has the potential to create something; and, the greater the gift, the more profound is the thing that they create.[2] Where does that come from? You cannot deliberately, cognitively set out to make something beautiful. (Well, yes, you can, actually.) What I mean is, at the moment you judge whether it is beautiful or not—either the shape of something, the color of something, the flow of a bit of text, a melody—some deeper force comes in to inform the response.

Stravinsky told us he invented at the piano. He called himself an inventor of music. Fine. But, what finally caused Stravinsky to invent the opening chord of *Symphony of Palms*? How many zillions of E minor chords are there in the world of music, and yet, that particular E minor chord, the way it is spaced, its voicing with all those doublings of the minor third, is unique to Igor Stravinsky. Hear that chord, and you know exactly that it's the opening chord of the *Symphony of Psalms*. And so, who or what told Stravinsky that this was the right sonority—did he figure it out? No, I don't think so. He may indeed have tried any number of sonorities, but he knew when he found it, and the result was creation, not just discovery. To, so to speak, keep trying things until you hear it—this is what yours truly does on a low, low, level when I'm doing an arrangement. I just try stuff until I hear it's right. I work until my ear says, "Yeah, that's how it should go."

Why, then, is "truth" a little imperfect? Why is it that when we listen to recordings of gripping live performances, we hear imperfections? Yet, if you listen to a CD of a controlled recording, that "perfect performance" is often stale and uninteresting.

Because we are only mortals. Because in the moment of actual doing, there will be a little slippage. The sanitizing process creates that so-called "perfect" recording. Of course, the ideal is that a performance will have that same technical perfection, *as well as* a sense of freedom and spontaneity. But, maybe that's just impossible, because it is so often true that the performances that speak most profoundly are in fact a bit untidy. Blemishes will almost inevitably happen in a live performance.

What would you like your legacy to be?

My hope that some people will have become more in touch with their innermost humanity: students, singers, people that I've worked with.

And are you aware that it could very well include hundreds of thousands of listeners that you've touched?

Maybe. I can't speak to that. But I do hope that I've made a difference through my ability to move people more deeply into themselves through the experience of making music together.

With respect to conducting students, I have succeeded if I have helped even a few of them overcome personal hurdles, to be able to just listen . . . and breathe.

NOTES

1. Flummerfelt has a very large collection of Santa Claus imagery: prints, carvings, needlepoint, paintings, metal works, pillows, and other media. He also collects quilts, an art rooted in craft and practical artisanry.

2. Wassily Kandinsky touches on this in his book *The Art of Spiritual Harmony*, trans. M. T. H. Sadler (London: Constable, 1914; reprinted as *Concerning the Spiritual in Art*, Dover, 1977):

> The inner need is built up of three mystical elements: (1) Every artist, as a creator has something in him which calls for expression (this is the element of personality). (2) Every artist, as child of his age, is impelled to express the spirit of his age (this is the element of style)—dictated by the period and particular country to which the artist belongs (it is doubtful how long the latter distinction will continue to exist). (3) Every artist, as a servant of art, has to help the cause of art (this is the element of pure artistry, which is constant in all ages and among all nationalities). (66)

Appendix A

BIOGRAPHICAL HIGHLIGHTS

The greater portion of the timeline is arranged by performing season—September through July, including Spoleto USA in May and Il Festival dei Due Mondi in June/July. Westminster Choir College activities are generally limited to the appearances of the Westminster Symphonic Choir and are listed in the order performed within each season. Performances of the New York Choral Artists are not included.

1937 February 24: Born to Mr. and Mrs. Ross Flummerfelt, Good Samaritan Hospital, Vincennes, Indiana.

1954 Graduated from Lincoln High School, Vincennes, Indiana.

1958 Bachelor of Music, DePauw University, Organ and Church Music. Summer Study, Julius Herford and Roger Wagner, San Diego, California.

1958–1960 Music Staff and University Organist, Purdue University.

1962 Master of Music, Philadelphia Conservatory of Music, Choral Conducting.

1963–1964 Instructor in Choral Music, University of Illinois. Summer Study, Nadia Boulanger, Fontainebleau, France.

1964–1968 Director of Choral Activities, DePauw University.

1968–1971 Director of Choral Activities, Florida State University.

1971–1993   *Maestro del Coro*, Il Festival dei Due Mondi, Spoleto, Italy (Gian Carlo Menotti, founder).

1971–2004   Artistic Director and Principal Conductor, Westminster Choir College.

1971–present   Principal Choral Director, New York Philharmonic.

1971–1972   Doctor of Musical Arts, University of Illinois, Choral Conducting.
Westminster Symphonic Choir
Latrobe's *The Dawn of Glory*. Nicholas Harsanyi, Piedmont Chamber Orchestra.
Bach's *St. John Passion*. Meredith Davies, New York Philharmonic and American Bible Society.
Liszt's *Psalm XIII*. Leonard Bernstein, New York Philharmonic.
Liszt's *A Faust Symphony*. Leonard Bernstein, New York Philharmonic.
Schubert's Mass in E-Flat. Ling Tung, Philadelphia Phiharmonia.

1972–1973
Westminster Symphonic Choir
Messiaen's *The Transformation of our Lord Jesus Christ*. Antal Doráti, National Symphony.
Verdi's *Aida*. William Smith, Trenton Symphony.
Liszt's *Missa solemnis*. Loren Maazel, New York Philharmonic.
Bach's *St. Matthew Passion*. Robert Shaw, Concerto Soloists of Philadelphia.
Berlioz's *Te Deum*. Pierre Boulez, New York Philharmonic.
Bartók's *Cantata Profana*. Pierre Boulez, New York Philharmonic.
Vivaldi's *Gloria*. James Loughran, New York Philharmonic and American Bible Society.
Handel's *Zadok the Priest*. James Loughran, New York Philharmonic and American Bible Society.
Mozart's *Coronation Mass*. James Loughran, New York Philharmonic and American Bible Society.
Mozart's *Vesperae Solemnes de Confessore in C*. James Loughran, New York Philharmonic and American Bible Society.

Mahler's Symphony no. 2. William Steinberg, Boston Symphony.
Penderecki's *St. Luke Passion*. Antal Doráti, National Symphony.

1973–1974   Le Prix de President de la Republique, L'Academie de
Disque Français, for Messiaen's *Transfiguration of Our Lord Jesus Christ*.
Westminster Symphonic Choir
Stravinsky's *Symphony of Psalms*. Antal Doráti, National Symphony.
Kodaly's *Psalmus Hungaricus*. Antal Doráti, National Symphony.
Bernstein's *Chichester Psalms*. Antal Doráti, National Symphony.
Beethoven's *Missa solemnis*. William Steinberg, Pittsburgh Symphony.

1975–1976   Mobil Oil Italia Pegasus Award, for his remarkable contribution to the Festival dei Due Mondi, Spoleto, Italy.
Westminster Symphonic Choir
Beethoven's Symphony no. 9. Pierre Boulez, New York Philharmonic.
Wagner's *Das Liebesmahl der Apostel*. Pierre Boulez, New York Philharmonic.
W. Schuman's *Casey at the Bat*. Antal Doráti, National Symphony.
Berlioz's *Roméo et Juliette*. William Steinberg, Pittsburgh Symphony.
Beethoven's *Missa solemnis*. Robert Shaw, Atlanta Symphony.
Berlioz's *Requiem*. Seiji Ozawa, Boston Symphony.

1976–1977
Westminster Symphonic Choir
Haydn's Mass in B-Flat (*Harmoniemesse*). Leonard Bernstein, New York Philharmonic.
Mahler's Symphony no. 2. James Levine, New York Philharmonic.
Mahler's Symphony no. 8. James Levine, New York Philharmonic.
Haydn's Mass in D Minor (*Lord Nelson Mass*). Leonard Bernstein, New York Philharmonic.
Poulenc's *Gloria*. Leonard Bernstein, New York Philharmonic.
Penderecki's *Magnificat*. Krzysztof Penderecki, Yale Philharmonic.
Berlioz's *The Damnation of Faust*. Pierre Boulez, New York Philharmonic.

1977–present   Artistic Director of Choral Activities, Spoleto Festival
USA, Charleston, South Carolina.

1977–1978

Westminster Symphonic Choir

Stravinsky's *Symphony of Psalms*. Leonard Bernstein, New York Philharmonic.

Haydn's Mass in B-Flat (*Theresienmesse*). Leonard Bernstein, New York Philharmonic.

Foss's *American Cantata*. Leonard Bernstein, New York Philharmonic.

Beethoven's *Missa solemnis*. Rafael Kubelik, New York Philharmonic.

Bach's *Six Motets* (The Westminster Choir). Wilhelm Ehmann, Concerto Soloists of Philadelphia.

Bach's Mass in B Minor. Joseph Flummerfelt, Holy Trinity Bach Orchestra.

1978–1979 Grammy nomination, Best Choral Performance, Classical, for Haydn's Mass No. 9 in D Minor (*Lord Nelson Mass*). The Westminster Symphonic Choir, Leonard Bernstein and the New York Philharmonic.

Westminster Symphonic Choir

Schubert's Mass in A-Flat. Zubin Mehta, New York Philharmonic.

Bruckner's *Te Deum*. Zubin Mehta, New York Philharmonic.

R. Strauss's *Burger aus Edelmann*. Erich Leinsdorf, New York Philharmonic.

Bernstein's *Chichester Psalms*. Zubin Mehta, New York Philharmonic.

Verdi's *Quatro pezzi sacri*. Zubin Mehta, New York Philharmonic.

Sibelius's *Kullervo*. Kenneth Schermerhorn, Milwaukee Symphony Orchestra.

1979–present Founder and Conductor, New York Choral Artists.

1979–1980

Westminster Symphonic Choir

Mendelssohn's *Elijah*. Zubin Mehta, New York Philharmonic.

Brahms's *Ein Deutches Requiem*. Erich Leinsdorf, New York Philharmonic.

Verdi's *Requiem* (Live from Lincoln Center). Zubin Mehta, New York Philharmonic.

Berlioz's *Roméo et Juliette*. Daniel Barenboim, New York Philharmonic.

Beethoven's Symphony no. 9. Rafael Kubelik, New York Philharmonic.

Berlioz's *Te Deum.* Zubin Mehta, New York Philharmonic.

Penderecki's *Dies irae.* (Auschwitz Oratorio), Zubin Mehta, New York Philharmonic.

Penderecki's *Lacrymosa.* Zubin Mehta, New York Philharmonic.

Bach's Cantata no. 50. Zubin Mehta, New York Philharmonic.

Bach's Cantatas (The Westminster Choir). Flummerfelt/Sheinkman, Bach Festival Orchestra.

1981–1982
Westminster Symphonic Choir
Mahler's Symphony no. 2. Zubin Mehta, New York Symphony.
Handel's *Messiah.* Thomas Michalak, New Jersey Symphony.
Beethoven's Symphony no. 9. Daniel Barenboim, L'Orchestre de Paris.
Handel's *Israel in Egypt.* Stephen Simon, Handel Festival Orchestra.

1982–1983   Honorary doctoral degree, DePauw University, Greencastle, Indiana.
Westminster Symphonic Choir
Mahler's Symphony no. 2. Gilbert Kaplan, American Symphony Orchestra.
Liszt's *A Faust Symphony.* Riccardo Muti, Philadelphia Orchestra.
Brahms's *Ein Deutsches Requiem.* Carlo Maria Giulini, Los Angeles Philharmonic.
A Festival of Christmas. Joseph Flummerfelt, New Jersey Symphony.
International Heinrich Schütz Festival. Joseph Flummerfelt/Wilhelm Ehmann.
Beethoven's Symphony no. 9. Robert Shaw, Atlanta Symphony.
Schoenberg's *Gurrelieder.* Zubin Mehta, New York Philharmonic.

1983–1984   Inclusion in *Baker's Biographical Dictionary of Musicians*, 7th edition.
Westminster Symphonic Choir
Verdi's *Macbeth.* Riccardo Muti, Philadelphia Orchestra.
Orff's *Carmina Burana.* Riccardo Muti, Philadelphia Orchestra.
Beethoven's Symphony no. 9. Michael Pratt, Princeton University Orchestra.

Brahms's *Ein Deutsches Requiem*. Robert Shaw, New York Philharmonic.

1984–1986　Member of the Choral Panel, National Endowment of the Arts.

1984–1985　Honorary doctoral degree, Purdue University, West Lafayette, Indiana.
Westminster Symphonic Choir
Gluck's *Orfeo et Euridice*. Riccardo Muti, Philadelphia Orchestra.
Scriabin's Symphony no. 1. Riccardo Muti, Philadelphia Orchestra.
Handel's *Ode to Saint Cecilia*. Kurt Masur, New York Philharmonic.
Handel's *Coronation Anthem no. 2*. Kurt Masur, New York Philharmonic.
Bach's *Magnificat*. Rafael Kubelik, New York Philharmonic.
Bach's Cantata no. 50. Rafael Kubelik, New York Philharmonic.

1985–1986　Honorary doctoral degree, Ursinus College, Collegeville, Pennsylvania. Grammy nomination, Best Choral Performance, Classical, for Berlioz's *Roméo et Juliette*. The Westminster Symphonic Choir, Riccardo Muti and the Philadelphia Orchestra.
Westminster Symphonic Choir
Verdi's *Rigoletto*. Riccardo Muti, Philadelphia Orchestra.
Berlioz's *Roméo et Juliette*. Riccardo Muti, Philadelphia Orchestra.
Brahms's *Ein Deutsches Requiem*. Kurt Masur, Gewandhaus Orchestra.
Duruflé's *Requiem*. Joseph Flummerfelt.

1986–1987
Westminster Symphonic Choir
Wagner's *Der Fliegende Holländer*. Riccardo Muti, Philadelphia Orchestra.
Beethoven's Symphony no. 9. Claudio Abbado, Vienna Philharmonic.
Britten's *War Requiem*. Mstislav Rostropovich, New York Philharmonic.
Mahler's Symphony no. 2. Leonard Bernstein, New York Philharmonic.

1987–1988   Visiting Professor, Indiana University. Distinguished Alumni Award, DePauw University, Greencastle, Indiana. Honorary doctoral degree, Vincennes University, Vincennes, Indiana.
Performance Highlight
Haydn's *The Creation.* New York Choral Artists, Joseph Flummerfelt and the New York Philharmonic.

Westminster Symphonic Choir
Fauré's *Requiem.* Leonard Slatkin, New York Philharmonic.
Verdi's *Quattro pezzi sacri.* Riccardo Muti, Philadelphia Orchestra.
Bruckner's *Te Deum.* Riccardo Muti, Philadelphia Orchestra.
Mozart's *Ave verum corpus.* Riccardo Muti, Philadelphia Orchestra.
Beethoven's Symphony no. 9. Riccardo Muti, Philadelphia Orchestra.

1988–1989
Westminster Symphonic Choir
Bruckner's *Te Deum.* Zubin Mehta, New York Philharmonic.
Bernstein's *Chichester Psalms.* Leonard Bernstein, New York Philharmonic.
Verdi's *Nabucco.* Riccardo Muti, Philadelphia Orchestra.
Stravinsky's *Symphony of Psalms.* Hugh Wolff, New Jersey Symphony.
Brahms's *Nänie.* Hugh Wolff, New Jersey Symphony.

1989–1990
Westminster Symphonic Choir
Britten's *War Requiem.* Hugh Wolff, New Jersey Symphony.
Brahms's *Alto Rhapsody.* Zubin Mehta, New York Philharmonic.
Stravinsky's *Oedipus Rex.* Zubin Mehta, New York Philharmonic.
Cherubini's *Requiem.* Riccardo Muti, Philadelphia Orchestra.
Pergolesi's *Stabat Mater.* Riccardo Muti, Philadelphia Orchestra.
Beethoven's Mass in C. Joseph Flummerfelt, Westminster Festival Orchestra.

1990–1991
Performance Highlights
Handel's *Messiah.* The Westminster Choir, Joseph Flummerfelt and the Greater Trenton Symphony Orchestra.
Handel's *Messiah.* The Westminster Choir, Joseph Flummerfelt and the New Jersey Symphony Orchestra.

Bernstein's "Almighty Father"; "Adonai" (*Chichester Psalms*); "To What You Said" (*Songfest*). The Westminster Symphonic Choir, Michael Tilson Thomas and the Bernstein Memorial Orchestra, *Leonard Bernstein Memorial Concert*, Carnegie Hall.

Mozart's *Requiem*. The Westminster Choir, Joseph Flummerfelt and the Westminster Festival Orchestra, Festival dei Due Mondi, Spoleto, Italy.

Westminster Symphonic Choir

Mahler's Symphony no. 3. Zubin Mehta, New York Philharmonic.

Beethoven's Symphony no. 9. Otto-Werner Mueller, Juilliard Orchestra.

Stravinsky's *Symphony of Psalms*. Otto-Werner Mueller, Juilliard Orchestra.

Mendelssohn's *Elijah*. Kurt Masur, New York Philharmonic.

Mozart's *Davidde Penitente*. Zubin Mehta, New York Philharmonic.

Strauss's *Elektra*. Lorin Maazel, Vienna Philharmonic.

Puccini's *Tosca*. Riccardo Muti, Philadelphia Orchestra.

Carnegie Hall Centennial Celebration with Robert Shaw, Robert Shaw.

Mahler's Symphony no. 3. James Levine, Vienna Philharmonic.

1991–1992

Performance Highlights

Verdi's *Va pensiero*. The Westminster Symphonic Choir, Riccardo Muti and the Philadelphia Orchestra.

Lutkin's *The Lord Bless You and Keep You*. Joseph Flummerfelt and the Westminster Choir, *Muti Farewell Concert*.

Honegger's *King David*. The Westminster Choir, Joseph Flummerfelt and the Westminster Festival Orchestra.

Westminster Symphonic Choir

Mozart's *Requiem*. Riccardo Muti, Philadelphia Orchestra.

Petrassi's *Coro di morti*. Riccardo Muti, Philadelphia Orchestra.

Mozart's Mass in C Minor. Robert Shaw, New York Philharmonic.

Barber's *Prayers of Kierkegaard*. Robert Shaw, New York Philharmonic.

Leoncavallo's *I Pagliacci*. Riccardo Muti, Philadelphia Orchestra.

Verdi's *Requiem*. Hugh Wolff, New Jersey Symphony.

1992–1993

Performance Highlights

Floyd's *A Time to Dance*. The Westminster Choir, Joseph Flummerfelt and the San Antonio Symphony, World Premiere at ACDA Convention, San Antonio.

Brahms's *Requiem*. The Westminster Symphonic Choir, Joseph Flummerfelt and the Westminster Festival Orchestra.

Westminster Symphonic Choir

Orff's *Carmina Burana*. Robert Spano, New Jersey Symphony.

Bach's *St. Matthew Passion*. Kurt Masur, New York Philharmonic.

Orff's *Carmina Burana*. Zdeněk Mácal, Philadelphia Orchestra.

1993–1994

Performance Highlights

Christmas at Carnegie Hall. The Westminster Choir with guest soloist Jennifer Larmore, Joseph Flummerfelt and the Orchestra of St. Luke's.

Haydn's Symphony no. 100 and Mass in D Minor (*Lord Nelson Mass*). The Westminster Choir, Joseph Flummerfelt and the New Jersey Symphony Orchestra.

Haydn's Mass in D Minor (*Lord Nelson Mass*); Handel's *Zadok the Priest*. The Westminster Choir, Joseph Flummerfelt and the Spoleto Festival Orchestra, Spoleto Festival USA.

Handel's *Acis and Galatea* (staged). Musical Director and Conductor, Joseph Flummerfelt and the Spoleto Festival Orchestra, Spoleto Festival USA.

Westminster Symphonic Choir

Britten's *War Requiem*. Wolfgang Sawallisch, Philadelphia Orchestra.

Dvořák's *Stabat Mater*. Zdeněk Mácal, New Jersey Symphony.

Honegger's *Jeanne D'Arc au Bucher*. Kurt Masur, New York Philharmonic.

1994–1999   Music Director, Singing City, Philadelphia, Pennsylvania.

1994–1995

Performance Highlights

Bach's Mass in B Minor. The Westminster Choir, Joseph Flummerfelt and the New Jersey Symphony.

Christmas at Carnegie Hall. The Westminster Choir with guest soloist George Shearing, Joseph Flummerfelt and the Orchestra of St.
Luke's.

Brahms's *Ein Deutches Requiem.* The Westminster Choir, Joseph Flummerfelt and the Spoleto Festival Orchestra, Spoleto Festival USA.

Westminster Symphonic Choir
Bernstein's *Chichester Psalms.* Joseph Flummerfelt, Orchestra of St.
Luke's.

Brahms's *Ein Deutsches Requiem.* Kurt Masur, New York Philharmonic.

Brahms's *Schicksalslied.* Kurt Masur, New York Philharmonic.

1995–1996

Performance Highlights
Christmas at Carnegie Hall. The Westminster Choir with guest solo-
ist George Shearing, Joseph Flummerfelt and the Orchestra of St.
Luke's.

*Concert in Celebration of Joseph Flummerfelt's Twenty-fifth Anniversary as
Conductor of the Westminster Symphonic Choir.* Joseph Flummerfelt,
conductor; Nancianne Parrella, organ; Westminster Festival Brass.

Westminster Symphonic Choir
Hindemith's *When Lilacs Last in the Dooryard Bloom'd.* Wolfgang
Sawallisch, Philadelphia Orchestra.

Stravinsky's *Symphony of Psalms.* Esa-Pekka Salonen, Los Angeles
Philharmonic.

Bach's *St. John Passion.* Helmuth Rilling, Philadelphia Orchestra.

1996–1997

Performance Highlights
Poulenc's *Gloria.* The Westminster Symphonic Choir, Joseph Flummerfelt and the Orchestra of St. Luke's, *Christmas at Carnegie Hall.*

Verdi's *Requiem.* The Westminster Choir and the Charleston Symphony Orchestra Chorus, Joseph Flummerfelt and the Spoleto
Festival Orchestra, Spoleto Festival USA.

Britten's *Curlew River* (Musical Director), Spoleto Festival USA.

Westminster Symphonic Choir
Mussorgsky/Schebalin's "Dream of the Peasant Grischko (Night on
Bald Mountain)" from *The Fair of Sorotchinsky.* Zdeněk Mácal, New
Jersey Symphony.

Britten's *War Requiem.* Kurt Masur, New York Philharmonic.
Debussy's *Le martyre de Saint Sebastien.* Kurt Masur, New York Philharmonic.

1997–1998
Performance Highlights
Bach's *St. John Passion.* The Westminster Choir, Joseph Flummerfelt
and the New Jersey Symphony Orchestra.
Bach's *Magnificat.* The Westminster Choir, Joseph Flummerfelt and
the Orchestra of St. Luke's, *Christmas at Carnegie Hall.*
Bach's *Magnificat* and Beethoven's Mass in C. The Westminster Choir
and the Charleston Symphony Orchestra Chorus, Joseph Flummerfelt and the Spoleto Festival Orchestra, Spoleto Festival USA.

Westminster Symphonic Choir
Beethoven's Symphony no. 9. Zdeněk Macal, New Jersey Sym-
phony.
Orff's *Carmina Burana.* Zdeněk Mácal, New Jersey Symphony.
Mahler's Symphony no. 3. Zdeněk Mácal, New Jersey Symphony.
Mendelssohn's *Elijah.* Kurt Masur, New York Philharmonic.
Bach's *Magnificat.* Wolfgang Sawallisch, Philadelphia Orchestra.
Orff's *Carmina Burana.* Zdeněk Mácal, New Jersey Symphony.

1998–1999
Performance Highlights
Haydn's Mass in D Minor (*Lord Nelson Mass*) and Duruflé's *Requiem.*
The Westminster Choir and the Charleston Symphony Orchestra
Chorus, Joseph Flummerfelt and the Spoleto Festival Orchestra,
Spoleto Festival USA.

Westminster Symphonic Choir
Beethoven's Symphony no. 9. Kurt Masur, New York Philhar-
monic.
Mahler's Symphony no. 3. Claudio Abbado, Berlin Philharmonic.
Debussy's *Three Nocturnes.* Claudio Abbado, Berlin Philharmonic.
Mendelssohn's *Elijah.* Wolfgang Sawallisch, Philadelphia Orchestra.
Duruflé's *Requiem.* Joseph Flummerfelt, Festival Orchestra.
Vaughan Williams's *Fantasia on Christmas Carols.* Joseph Flummerfelt,
Orchestra of St. Luke's.
Beethoven's Symphony no. 9. Mark Laycock, Princeton Chamber
Symphony.

Beethoven's *Calm Sea and Prosperous Voyage*. Mark Laycock, Princeton Chamber Symphony.

1999–2000

Performance Highlights

Brahms's *Ein Deutches Requiem*. The Westminster Symphonic Choir, Joseph Flummerfelt and the Westminster Festival Orchestra.

Poulenc's *Mass in G* and *Organ Concerto*. The Westminster Choir, Joseph Flummerfelt, Poulenc Centennial Festival, New York City and St. Ignatius Orchestra.

Brahms's *Alto Rhapsody* and *Schicksalslied*; Poulenc's *Gloria*. The Westminster Choir and the Charleston Symphony Orchestra Chorus, Joseph Flummerfelt and the Spoleto Festival Orchestra, Spoleto Festival USA.

Westminster Symphonic Choir

Dvořák's *Requiem*. Zdeněk Mácal, New Jersey Symphony Orchestra.

Saariaho's *Oltra mar: Seven Preludes for the New Millennium*. Kurt Masur, New York Philharmonic.

Brahms's *Ein Deutsches Requiem*. Joseph Flummerfelt, Festival Orchestra.

Bach's *St. John Passion*. Kurt Masur, New York Philharmonic.

Adès's *America: A prophecy*. Kurt Masur, New York Philharmonic.

2000–2001

Performance Highlights

Paulus's *Voices of Light*. The Westminster Choir, Joseph Flummerfelt and the New York Philharmonic, World Premiere.

Mozart's *Requiem* and Stravinsky's *Symphony of Psalms*. The Westminster Choir and the Charleston Symphony Orchestra Chorus, Joseph Flummerfelt and the Spoleto Festival Orchestra, Spoleto Festival USA.

Westminster Symphonic Choir

Mendelssohn's *St. Paul*. Kurt Masur, New York Philharmonic.

Beethoven's *Missa solemnis*. Wolfgang Sawallisch, Philadelphia Orchestra.

Elgar's *The Dream of Gerontius*. Sir Colin Davis, New York Philharmonic.

2001–2002

Performance Highlights

Honegger's *King David* and Bernstein's *Chichester Psalms*. The Westminster Choir and the Charleston Symphony Chorus, Joseph Flummerfelt and the Spoleto Festival Orchestra, Spoleto Festival USA.

Westminster Symphonic Choir
Dvořák's *The Spectre's Bride*. Zdeněk Mácal, New Jersey Symphony Orchestra.
Mahler's Symphony no. 3. Mariss Jansons, New York Philharmonic.
Mahler's Symphony no. 2. Riccardo Chailly, Royal Concertgebouw Orchestra.
Verdi's *Requiem*. Riccardo Muti, New York Philharmonic.

2002–2003
Performance Highlights
Verdi's *Requiem*. Hartford Chorale, Joseph Flummerfelt and the Hartford Symphony.
Brahms's Concerto in A minor for Violin and Cello, op. 102 and Mozart's *Requiem*. Sewanee Church Music Conference Festival Chorus, Joseph Flummerfelt and the Sewanee Festival Orchestra, Sewanee Summer Music Festival.
Wagner's "Prelude" and "Liebestod" from *Tristan und Isolde* and Elgar's *Enigma Variations*. Joseph Flummerfelt and the Sewanee Symphony, Sewanee Summer Music Festival.
Haydn's Mass in B-Flat (*Theresienmesse*) and Verdi's *Stabat Mater* and *Te Deum*. The Westminster Choir and the Charleston Symphony Chorus, Joseph Flummerfelt and the Spoleto Festival Orchestra, Spoleto Festival USA.

Westminster Symphonic Choir
Verdi's *Requiem*. Zdeněk Mácal, New Jersey Symphony Orchestra.
Dvořák's *Te Deum*. Zdeněk Mácal, New Jersey Symphony Orchestra.
Dvořák's *Psalm 149*. Zdeněk Mácal, New Jersey Symphony Orchestra.
Dvořák's *Amid Nature*. Zdeněk Mácal, New Jersey Symphony Orchestra.
Mahler's Symphony no. 3. Michael Tilson Thomas, San Francisco Symphony Orchestra.
Handel's *Messiah*. Sir Neville Marriner, New York Philharmonic.
Berlioz's *Requiem*. Charles Dutoit, New York Philharmonic.

Fauré's *Requiem*. Joseph Flummerfelt, New Jersey Symphony Orchestra.

Haydn's Mass in B-Flat (*Theresienmesse*). Joseph Flummerfelt, New Jersey Symphony Orchestra.

Berlioz's *Béatrice et Bénédict*. Sir Colin Davis, New York Philharmonic.

2003–2004 Conductor of the Year, 2004, Musical America. Grammy Award, Best Classical Performance, for John Adams's *On the Transmigration of Souls*. Lorin Maazel and the New York Philharmonic.

Performance Highlight
Vaughan Williams's *Serenade to Music, Five Mystical Songs, Dona nobis pacem*. The Westminster Choir and the Charleston Symphony Chorus, Joseph Flummerfelt and the Spoleto Festival Orchestra, Spoleto Festival USA.

Westminster Symphonic Choir
Beethoven's Symphony no. 9. Lorin Maazel, New York Philharmonic.

Berlioz's *Sara la Baigneuse*. Sir Colin Davis, New York Philharmonic.

Berlioz's *Tristis*. Sir Colin Davis, New York Philharmonic.

A Thanksgiving Festival. Joseph Flummerfelt, Westminster Festival Orchestra.

Handel's *Messiah*. Nicholas McGegan, New York Philharmonic.

Bartók's *Miraculous Mandarin*. Pierre Boulez, Cleveland Orchestra.

Wagner's *Parsifal* (Act II). Pierre Boulez, Cleveland Orchestra.

Beethoven's *Missa solemnis*. Joseph Flummerfelt, Westminster Festival Orchestra.

Bernstein's *Candide* (concert version). Marin Alsop, New York Philharmonic.

Mahler's Symphony no. 3. Lorin Maazel, New York Philharmonic.

2005 DePauw University Gold Medal, Greencastle, Indiana; highest alumni award. Guest conductor with a professional choir in Seoul, South Korea. Guest conductor, Indiana ACDA State Convention.

Performance Highlights
Fauré's *Requiem* and Stravinsky's *Symphony of Psalms*. Joseph Flummerfelt in residence at DePauw University.

Fauré's *Requiem* and Duruflé's *Requiem*. Joseph Flummerfelt and the Montgomery Choral Society, Montgomery, Alabama.

Brahms's *Ein Deutsches Requiem*. The Westminster Choir and the Charleston Symphony Chorus, Joseph Flummerfelt and the Spoleto Festival Orchestra, Spoleto Festival USA.

Fauré's *Requiem* and Duruflé's *Requiem*. Joseph Flummerfelt and the Mendelssohn Choir of Pittsburgh.

Schumann's *Spanisches Liederspiel* and *Liebeslieder*. Joseph Flummerfelt and the Boston University Chamber Chorus and Women's Chorale, in residence at Boston University.

2006   Guest Artist, Eastman Summer Choral Master Classes, Rochester, New York.

Performance Highlights

Barber, Schoenberg, Verdi, Lauridsen, and Brahms. Joseph Flummerfelt and the Formosa Singers, Taipei, Taiwan.

Christmas at Esplanade. Joseph Flummerfelt and Philharmonic Chamber Choir, Singapore.

2007   Master Teacher, Chorus America workshop, San Francisco, California. Guest Conductor, Illinois State ACDA Convention. Sunday broadcast, Joseph Flummerfelt with the Mormon Tabernacle Choir.

Performance Highlights

Fauré's *Requiem* and choral classics. Joseph Flummerfelt in residence at Sam Houston State University, Huntsville, Texas.

2008   Guest Conductor, Festival of American Choral Music, Houston Chamber Choir. Conducting master classes, University of Illinois at Urbana-Champaign. Conductor, Collegiate Honor Choir, Central Division, ACDA Convention, Grand Rapids, Michigan. Conducting master classes, National Conservatory of Music, Sofia, Bulgaria.

Performance Highlights

Poulenc's Mass in G and other choral selections. Joseph Flummerfelt and the Formosa Singers, Taipei, Taiwan.

American Choral Classics. Joseph Flummerfelt and the New York Choral Artists, Gettysburg Festival, Gettysburg, Pennsylvania.

Fauré's *Requiem*, R. Strauss's *Five Songs for Soprano and Orchestra*, and Mahler's *Rückert-Lieder*. Joseph Flummerfelt and the Calgary Philharmonic Orchestra and Chorus, Calgary, Alberta.

2009 Conducting master classes, University of Illinois at Urbana-Champaign. Guest Conductor, UTA Chamber Singers and Concert Chorale,

Austin, Texas. In residence, University of Texas at Austin, Butler School
of Music, Distinguished Teacher Series. Guest Artist, Eastman Summer
Choral Master Classes, Rochester, New York.

Performance Highlights

Brahms's *Ein Deutches Requiem.* Joseph Flummerfelt and the University
   of Illinois Orchestra and Choruses, in residence at University of Illinois at Urbana-Champaign.

Poulenc's *Gloria* and Mozart's *Requiem.* Joseph Flummerfelt conducting the Westminster Choir, the Charleston Symphony Chorus, and
   the Spoleto Festival Orchestra, Spoleto Festival USA.

Appendix B

COLLABORATING ORCHESTRAS
AND CONDUCTORS

This appendix contains a representative list of those with whom Flummerfelt has worked.

CONDUCTORS

Claudio Abbado
Spiros Argiris
Daniel Barenboim
Leonard Bernstein
Pierre Boulez
Riccardo Chailley
Sir Colin Davis
Christoph von Dohnányi
Antal Doráti
Charles Dutoit
Alan Gilbert
Carlo Maria Giulini
Christopher Keene
Rafael Kubelik
Erich Leinsdorf
James Levine
Lorin Maazel
Zdeněk Mácal
Sir Neville Marriner
Kurt Masur
Nicholas McGegan

Zubin Mehta
Riccardo Muti
Roger Norrington
Seiji Ozawa
Krzysztof Penderecki
Helmuth Rilling
Esa-Pekka Salonen
Wolfgang Sawallisch
Thomas Schippers
Robert Shaw
Leonard Slatkin
William Steinberg
Michael Tilson Thomas
Roger Wagner

ORCHESTRAS CONDUCTED

Calgary Symphony
Hartford Symphony
Fort Worth Symphony
New Jersey Symphony
New York Philharmonic
Orchestra of St. Luke's
Phoenix Symphony
San Antonio Symphony
Spoleto Festival Orchestra

ORCHESTRAS WITH WHICH
FLUMMERFELT'S CHOIRS HAVE SUNG

American

Boston Symphony
Los Angeles Philharmonic
National Symphony
New Jersey Symphony
New York Philharmonic
Orchestra of St. Luke's

Philadelphia Orchestra
Pittsburg Symphony
San Antonio Symphony
San Francisco Symphony

European

Berlin Philharmonic
Gewandhaus Orchestra, Leipzig
Orchestre de Paris
Royal Concertgebouw Orchestra, Amsterdam
Vienna Philharmonic

DISCOGRAPHY

These recordings are listed by composer's name, with compilations at the end of the list.

Adams, John: *On the Transmigration of Souls*

CD: Nonesuch Records (NON 79816)
Release date: 2007
2005 Grammy Award Winner for Best Classical Contemporary Composition; Classical Album of the Year; Best Orchestral Performance
New York Choral Artists
Brooklyn Youth Chorus
New York Philharmonic
Lorin Maazel, conductor
Preben Antonson, boy soprano; Philip Smith, trumpet

Barber, Samuel: *Antony & Cleopatra*

CD (2 discs): New World Records (NWR 80322)
Release date: 1983
1985 Grammy Award Winner for Best New Classical Composition
Westminster Choir
Spoleto Festival Orchestra
Christian Badea, conductor
Esther Hinds, Cleopatra; Jeffrey Wells, Antony; Kathryn Cowdrick, Charmian; Jane Bunnell, Iras; Eric Halfvarson, Enobarbus; Robert Grayson, Caesar; Mark Cleveland, Maecenas; Charles Damsel, Agrippa/Second Guard; Steven Cole, Messenger; David Hickox,

Eros; David Hamilton, Dolabella/Third Guard; Kent Weaver, Thidias; Ian Clark, Senator; Dale Stine, Alexas; Philip Skinner, Soothsayer/Fourth Guard/Rustic; Robert Swensen, First Guard/A Soldier of Caesar; Rob Phillips, First Soldier; Alan Arak, Second Soldier; David Dik, Guardsman

Beethoven, Ludwig van: *"Choral" Symphony no. 9; "Choral Fantasy"*

LP: RCA Records (LP)
Release date: 1983
"Choral" Symphony no. 9
    New York Choral Artists
    New York Philharmonic
    Zubin Mehta, conductor
    Margaret Price, soprano; Marilyn Horne, mezzo-soprano; Jon Vickers, tenor; Matti Salminen, bass
"Choral Fantasy" (*Fantasia* in C Minor, op. 80)
    New York Choral Artists
    Zubin Mehta, conductor
    Emanuel Ax, piano

Beethoven, Ludwig van: *Beethoven—Greatest Hits*

CD: RCA Records (RCA 60831)
Release date: 1991
Tracks:
    6. Symphony no. 9 "Choral": presto/allegro assai
    8. *Fantasia* for piano, chorus, and orchestra ("Choral Fantasy"), op. 80 conclusion
See information under original release listing: RCA Records, 1983

Beethoven, Ludwig van: *Beethoven: Ninth Symphony*

CD: RCA Records (RCA 60477)
Release date: 1991
See information under original release listing: RCA Records, 1983

Beethoven, Ludwig van: *"Emperor" Piano Concerto no. 5; Choral Fantasia*

CD: RCA Records (RCA 61213)
Release date: 1992
See information under original release listing: RCA Records, 1983

Beethoven, Ludwig van: *Basic 100 Vol. 1—Beethoven: Symphony no. 9; Prometheus Overture*

CD: RCA Records (RCA 61550)
Release date: 1993
See information under original release listing: RCA Records, 1983

Beethoven, Ludwig van: *Egmont & The Ruins of Athens*

CD: Angel/EMI (EMI 315552)
Release date: 1994
New York Choral Artists
Orchestra of St. Luke's
Dennis Russell Davies, conductor
Mechthild Gessendorf, soprano; Roger Andrews, baritone

Beethoven, Ludwig van: *Beethoven: Complete Symphonies*

CD (6-CD boxed set): EMI Classics (EMI 729232A)
Release date: 1998
Disc 6, Track 4: Symphony no. 9 "Choral": "Ode to Joy"
See information under original release listing: Angel/EMI, 1998

Beethoven, Ludwig van: *Symphony no. 9*

CD: Angel/EMI (EMI 732842)
Release date: 1999
Westminster Symphonic Choir
Philadelphia Orchestra
Riccardo Muti, conductor
Cheryl Studer, soprano; Delores Ziegler, mezzo-soprano; Peter Seiffert, tenor; James Morris, bass

Beethoven, Ludwig van: *Best Classics 100*

CD (6-CD boxed set): EMI Classics (EMI 708532B)
Release date: 2006

Disc 1, Track 7: Symphony no. 9 "Choral": "Ode to Joy"
See information under original release listing: Angel/EMI, 1999

Beethoven, Ludwig van: *Best Beethoven 100*

CD (6-CD boxed set): EMI Classics (EMI 973072B)
Release date: 2007
Disc 1, Track 15: Symphony no. 9 "Choral": "Ode to Joy"
See information under original release listing: Angel/EMI, 1999

Berlioz, Hector: *Roméo et Juliette, Les nuits d'été*

LP: EMI Classics
Release date: 1986
1987 Grammy Nominee for Best Choral Performance
Westminster Symphonic Choir
Philadelphia Orchestra
Riccardo Muti, conductor
Jessye Norman, soprano; Janet Baker, mezzo-soprano; John Aler, tenor; Simon Estes, bass-baritone

Berlioz, Hector: *Roméo et Juliette, Les nuits d'été*

CD (2 discs): EMI Classics (EMI 176402B)
Release date: 2008
See information under original release listing: EMI Classics, 1986 (remastered for CD in 2008)

Brahms, Johannes: *Ein Deutsches Requiem*

CD: Teldec (TLD 98413)
Release date: 1995
Westminster Symphonic Choir
New York Philharmonic
Kurt Masur, conductor
Sylvia McNair, soprano; Håkan Hagegård, baritone

Brahms, Johannes: *Singing for Pleasure: The Westminster Choir Sings Brahms*

CD: Delos Records (DEL 3193)
Release date: 1996

The New York Times cited this CD as one of its five favorite Brahms recordings.
Tracks:
1. *Liebeslieder Waltzes*, op. 52, no. 8: "Wenn so lind dein Auge mir"
2. *Liebeslieder Waltzes*, op. 52, no. 9: "Am Donaustrande"
3. *Liebeslieder Waltzes*, op. 52, no, 10: "O wie sanft"
4. *Liebeslieder Waltzes*, op. 52, no. 11: "Nein, es ist nicht"
5. *Liebeslieder Waltzes*, op. 52, no. 12: "Schlosser auf"
6. *Liebeslieder Waltzes*, op. 52, no. 13: "Vögelein"
7. *Liebeslieder Waltzes*, op. 52, no. 14: "Sieh, wie ist"
8. *Liebeslieder Waltzes*, op. 52, no. 15: "Nachtigall"
9. *Liebeslieder Waltzes*, op. 52, no. 16: "Ein dunkler Schacht"
10. *Deutsche Volkslieder* for Chorus, WoO 34, no. 9: "Abschiedslied"
11. *Deutsche Volkslieder* for Chorus, WoO 34, no. 8: "In stiller Nacht"
12. *Deutsche Volkslieder* for Chorus, WoO 34, no. 11: "Die Wollust"
13. *Zigeunerlieder*, op. 103, no. 5: "Brauner Bursche führt zum Tanz"
14. *Zigeunerlieder*, op. 103, no. 6: "Röslein dreie in der Reihe"
15. *Zigeunerlieder*, op. 103, no. 7: "Kommt dir manchmal"
16. *Zigeunerlieder*, op. 103, no. 8: "Horch, der Wind klagt"
17. *Zigeunerlieder*, op. 103, no. 9: "Weit und breit schaut niemand"
18. Motets, op. 74, no. 2: "O Heiland, reiss die Himmel auf"
19. Vocal Quartets, op. 64, no. 1: "An die Heimat"
20. Vocal Quartets, op. 64, no. 2: "Der Abend"
21. Vocal Quartets, op. 92, no. 2: "Spätherbst"
22. Vocal Quartets, op. 92, no. 3: "Abendlied"
23. *Neue Liebeslieder Waltzes*, op. 65, no. 15: "Zum Schluss"
Westminster Choir
Joseph Flummerfelt, conductor
Glenn Parker and Nancianne Parrella, piano

Brahms, Johannes: *Symphony no. 4; Schicksalslied*

CD: Teldec (TLD 13695)
Release date: 1996
Track 5: *Hyperions Schicksalslied*, op. 54: "Langsam und sehnsuchts-voll"
Westminster Symphonic Choir
New York Philharmonic
Kurt Masur, conductor

Britten, Benjamin: *War Requiem*

CD (2 discs): Teldec (USA) (TLD 17115)
Release date: 1998
Westminster Symphonic Choir
American Boychoir
New York Philharmonic
Kurt Masur, conductor
Carol Vaness, soprano; Jerry Hadley, tenor; Thomas Hampson, baritone

Dvořák, Antonín: *Dvořák: Stabat Mater, etc.*

CD (2 discs): Delos Records (DEL 3161)
Release date: 1994
Stabat Mater, op. 58/B 71
    Westminster Symphonic Choir
    New Jersey Symphony Orchestra
    Zdeněk Mácal, conductor
    Kaaren Erickson, soprano; Claudine Carlson, mezzo-soprano; John Aler, tenor; John Cheek, bass
Biblical Songs, op. 99/B 185
    New Jersey Symphony Orchestra
    Zdeněk Mácal, conductor
    Manfred Hemm, bass

Dvořák, Antonín: *Requiem/Symphony 9*

CD (2 discs): Delos International (DEL 3260)
Release date: 2000

2000 Grammy Award Winner for Best Classical Engineered Album
New Jersey Symphony Orchestra
Westminster Symphonic Choir
Zdeněk Mácal, conductor
Oksana Krovystka, soprano; Wendy Hoffman, mezzo-soprano; John
Aler, tenor; Gustáv Belácek, bass

Gershwin, George: *Kiri Sings Gershwin*

LP: Angel/EMI
Release date: 1987
Tracks:
1. *George White's Scandals of 1924*: "Somebody Loves Me"
2. *Primrose*: "Boy Wanted"
3. *A Damsel in Distress*: "Things Are Looking Up"
4. *Goldwyn Follies*: "Love Walked In"
5. *Goldwyn Follies*: "Love Is Here To Stay"
6. *Oh, Kay!*: "Someone To Watch Over Me"
7. *Girl Crazy*: "But Not for Me"
8. *Porgy and Bess*: "Summertime"
9. *Strike Up the Band* (first version): "The Man I Love"
10. *Strike Up The Band* (second version): "Soon"
11. *Strike Up the Band* (first version): "Meadow Serenade"
12. *A Damsel in Distress*: "Nice Work If You Can Get It"
13. "By Strauss"
14. *Girl Crazy*: "Embraceable You"
15. *Girl Crazy*: "I Got Rhythm"
New York Choral Artists
New Princess Theater Orchestra
John McGlinn, conductor
Kiri Te Kanawa, soprano

Gershwin, George: *Kiri Sings Gershwin*

CD: Angel/EMI (EMI 47454)
Release date: 1990
See information under original LP release: Angel/EMI, 1987 (remas-
tered to CD in 1990)

Gershwin, George: *Of Thee I Sing/Let 'Em Eat Cake*

CD (2 discs): Sony (M2K 42522)
Release date: 1990
Disc 1: *Of Thee I Sing*
Tracks:
1. "Overture"
2. "Wintergreen for President"
3. "Who Is the Lucky Girl To Be?"
4. "Dimple on my Knee"
5. "Because, Because"
6. "Never Was There a Girl So Fair"
7. "Some Girls Can Bake a Pie"
8. "Love Is Sweeping the Country"
9. "Of Thee I Sing"
10. Finale Act 1/"Supreme Court Judges"
11. "Kiss for Cinderella"/ "Some Girls Can Bake a Pie" (Reprise)/ "Of Thee I Sing"
12. "Hello, Good Morning"
13. "Who Cares?"
14. "Illegitimate Daughter"/"Because, Because" (Reprise)
15. "Who Cares?" (Reprise)
16. "Senator from Minnesota"
17. "Senate"
18. "Jilted/I'm About To Be a Mother"
19. "Posterity Is Just Around the Corner"
20. "Trumpeter Blow Your Horn"
21. "Finale Ultimo"
22. "Of Thee I Sing" (Reprise)
Disc 2: *Let 'Em Eat Cake*
1. "Overture"
2. "Tweedledee for President"
3. "Union Square"
4. "Shirts by the Millions"
5. "Comes the Revolution"
6. "Mine"
7. "Climb Up the Social Ladder"
8. "Union League"
9. "On and On and On"
10. "Introduction"

11. "I've Brushed My Teeth"
12. "General's Gone to a Party"
13. "Mothers of the Nation"
14. "Let 'Em Eat Cake"
15. "Blue, Blue, Blue"
16. "Who's the Greatest?"
17. "League of the Nations"
18. "No Comprenez, No Capish, No Versteh!"
19. "When Nations Get Together"
20. "Why Speak of Money?"/ "Who's the Greatest" (Reprise)
21. "Up and at 'Em"
22. "That's What He Did"
23. "I Know a Foul Ball"
24. "Throttle Throttlebottom"
25. "It Isn't What You Did"
26. "Mine" (Reprise)
27. "First Lady and First Gent"
28. "Hanging Throttlebottom in the Morning"
29. "Fashion Show"
30. "Finale Ultimo: Of Thee I Sing (Reprise)"

New York Choral Artists
Orchestra of St. Luke's
Michael Tilson Thomas, conductor
Orchestrations by Robert Russell Bennett and Russell Warren
With George Dvorsky, Louise Edeiken, Jack Gilford, Merwin Gold-
smith, Walter Hook, Larry Kert, Frank Kopyc, Maureen McGov-
ern, Paige O'Hara, Casper Roos, Mark Zimmerman

Gershwin, George: *Rhapsody in Blue, Porgy and Bess (Excerpts)*

CD: Teldec (2292-46318-2; also released on Ultima (ERA 84518))
Release date: 1991
Tracks:

1. *Porgy and Bess*: "Introduction" and "Summertime"
2. *Porgy and Bess*: "A Woman Is a Sometime Thing"
3. *Porgy and Bess*: "Overflow"
4. *Porgy and Bess*: "Since I Lose My Man"
5. *Porgy and Bess*: "The Promise' Lan'"
6. *Porgy and Bess*: "I Got Plenty o' Nuttin'"
7. *Porgy and Bess*: "Bess: You Is My Woman Now"

8. *Porgy and Bess:* "I Can't Sit Down"
9. *Porgy and Bess:* "It Ain't Necessarily So"
10. *Porgy and Bess:* "There's a Boat Dat's Leavin' Soon for New York"
11. *Porgy and Bess:* "O, Lawd I'm on My Way"
12. "An American in Paris"
13. "Cuban Overture"

New York Choral Artists
New York Philharmonic
Zubin Mehta, conductor
Roberta Alexander, soprano; Gregg Baker, baritone

Gershwin, George: *Rhapsody in Blue, Porgy and Bess (Excerpts)*

CD: Ultima (ERA 84518)
Release date: 2000
See information under original release listing: Teldec, 1991
This 2-CD set includes additional Gershwin performances by the Monte Carlo Philharmonic Orchestra and pianists Michel Legrand and Gabriel Tacchino.

Haydn, Franz Joseph: *Mass in B-Flat major, H 22 no. 14 "Harmoniemesse"*

LP: Columbia (M-33267)
Release date: 1976
Westminster Symphonic Choir
New York Philharmonic
Leonard Bernstein, conductor
Judith Blegen, soprano; Frederica Von Stade, mezzo-soprano; Kenneth Riegel, tenor; Simon Estes, bass

Haydn, Franz Joseph: *Mass in D Minor, H. 22 no. 11 "Nelsonmesse"*

LP: Columbia (M-35100)
Release date: 1977
1979 Grammy Nominee for Best Classical Performance—Choral
Westminster Symphonic Choir
New York Philharmonic

Leonard Bernstein, conductor
Judith Blegen, soprano; Gwendolyn Killebrew, mezzo-soprano; Kenneth Riegel, tenor; Simon Estes, bass

Haydn, Franz Joseph: *Leonard Bernstein Conducts Haydn*

CD (12-CD boxed set): Sony Classical (SNYC 48045)
Release date: 2009
Disc 9: Mass in D Minor, H. 22 No. 11 *"Nelsonmesse"*
Disc 10: Mass in B-Flat Major, H. 22 No. 14 *"Harmoniemesse"*
See information under original LP release listing: Columbia, 1976/1977

Leoncavallo, Ruggero: *Pagliacci*

CD: Philips Classics (PHI 4381322)
Release date: 1993
Westminster Symphonic Choir
Philadelphia Boys Choir
Philadelphia Orchestra
Riccardo Muti, conductor
Luciano Pavarotti, Canio/Pagliaccio; Daniela Dessì, Nedda/Colombina; Juan Pons, Tonio/Taddeo; Paolo Coni, Silvio; Ernesto Gavazzi, Beppe/Arlecchino; David Newman, bass; Jonathan Boyd, tenor

Liszt, Franz: *A Faust Symphony*

CD: Angel/EMI (EMI 090172)
Release date: 1982
Westminster Choir
Philadelphia Orchestra
Riccardo Muti, conductor
Gösta Winbergh, tenor

Mahler, Gustav: *Symphony no. 2 in C "Resurrection"*

CD: Deutsche Grammophon (DGG 4233952)
Release date: 1990
Westminster Choir

New York Philharmonic
Leonard Bernstein, conductor
Barbara Hendricks, soprano; Christa Ludwig, mezzo-soprano

Mahler, Gustav: *Bernstein Collectors
Edition—Mahler I: Symphonies 1–4, etc.*

CD (6-CD boxed set): Deutsche Grammophon (DGG B000532202)
Release date: 2005
Disc 4: Symphony no. 2 in C Minor "Resurrection"
See information under original release listing: Deutsche Grammophon, 1990

Mahler, Gustav: *The Complete Mahler Symphonies,
Live: Symphony no. 2*

MP3 download: New York Philharmonic
Release date: 2009 (Recorded 2003)
New York Choral Artists
New York Philharmonic
Lorin Maazel, conductor
Jessica Jones, soprano; Cornelia Kallisch, mezzo-soprano

Mahler, Gustav: *Symphony no. 2 in C "Resurrection"*

DVD: Video Artists International (VAI DVD 4432)
Release date: 2007
New York Choral Artists
Riverside Chorale
Musicians of the New York Philharmonic, Detroit Symphony Orchestra, New Jersey Symphony, Metropolitan Opera Orchestra and Philadelphia Orchestra
Neeme Järvi, conductor
Twyla Robinson, soprano; Susanne Mentzer, mezzo-soprano
Produced and directed by Jason Starr

Mahler, Gustav: *Symphony no. 3 in D Minor*

CD: Deutsche Grammophon (DGG 4273282)
Release date: 1989

1990 Grammy Award Winner for Best Orchestral Performance
New York Choral Artists
Brooklyn Boys Chorus
New York Philharmonic
Leonard Bernstein, conductor
Christa Ludwig, mezzo-soprano

Mahler, Gustav: *The Complete Mahler Symphonies,*
Live: Symphony no. 3

MP3 download: New York Philharmonic
Release date: 2009 (Recorded 2003)
Women of the Westminster Symphonic Choir
American Boychoir
New York Philharmonic
Lorin Maazel, conductor
Anna Larsson, contralto

Mahler, Gustav: *Mahler: The Complete*
Symphonies & Orchestral Songs

CD (16-CD boxed set): Deutsche Grammophon (DGG 4590802)
Release date: 1998
Disc 2: Symphony no. 2 in C Minor "Resurrection"
Disc 3: Symphony no. 3 in D Minor
See information under original release listings: Deutsche Grammo-
phon, 1989; Deutsche Grammophon, 1990

Mahler, Gustav: *The Complete Mahler Symphonies, Live: Symphony*
no. 8

MP3 download: New York Philharmonic
Release date: 2009 (recorded 2009)
New York Choral Artists
The Dessoff Symphonic Choir
Brooklyn Youth Chorus
New York Philharmonic
Lorin Maazel, conductor
Christine Brewer, soprano (Magna Peccatrix); Nancy Gustafson, soprano
(Una Poenitentium); Jeanine DeBique, soprano (Mater gloriosa);

Mary Phillips, mezzo-soprano (Mulier Samaritana); Nancy Maultsby, mezzo-soprano (Maria Aegyptiaca); Anthony Dean Griffey, tenor (Doctor Marianus); Wolfgang Schöne, bass (Pater ecstaticus); Jason Grant, bass-baritone (Pater profundus)

Menotti, Gian Carlo: *Missa "O Pulchritudo"*

LP: Westminster Recording Label
Release date: 1981
Westminster Choir
Spoleto Festival Orchestra
Joseph Flummerfelt, conductor

Messiaen, Olivier: *La Transfiguration de Notre Seigneur Jésus-Christ*

LP: London/Decca (425 616-2)
Release date: 1975
Winner of Le Prix du President de le Republique, L'Academie de Disque Français
Westminster Symphonic Choir
National Symphony
Antal Doráti, conductor
Wallace Mann, flute; Loren Kitt, clarinet; János Starker, cello; Frank Ames, marimba; Ronald; Barnett, vibraphone; John Kane, xylorimba; Yvonne Loriod, piano
Michael Sylvester, tenor; Paul Aquino, baritone

Messiaen, Olivier: *La Transfiguration de Notre Seigneur Jésus-Christ*

CD (2 discs): London/Decca (DECCA 425616)
Release date: 1990
See information under original LP release listing: London/Decca 1975 (remastered onto CD in 1990)

Mussorgsky, Modest: *Heaven and Hell: Mácal Conducts Mussorgsky*

CD: Delos Records (DEL 3217)
Release date: 1997
Track 1: Modest Mussorgsky: *Sorochintsy Fair:* "The Peasant Lad's Dream Vision"
Westminster Symphonic Choir

New Jersey Symphony Orchestra
Zdeněk Mácal, conductor
Clayton Brainerd, bass-baritone

Poulenc, Francis: *Gloria*

LP: Columbia (M-34551)
Release date: 1977
Westminster Symphonic Choir
New York Philharmonic
Leonard Bernstein, conductor
Judith Blegen, soprano

Puccini, Giacomo: *Tosca*

CD (2 discs): Decca/Philips Classics (PHILIPS CD 434 595-2)
Release date: 2003
Westminster Symphonic Choir
Philadelphia Boys Choir
Philharmonia Orchestra
Riccardo Muti, conductor
Carol Vaness, Tosca; Giacomo Giacomini, Cavaradossi; Giorgio
    Zancanaro, Scarpia; Danilo Serraiocco, Angelotti; Alfredo Mari-
    otti, Sagrestano; Piero de Palma, Spoletta; Orazio Mori, Sciarrone;
    Charles Austin, Carceriere; Jeffrey Smith, Pastore

Scriabin, Alexander: *Scriabin: Symphonies, etc.*

CD (3 discs): EMI Classics (EMI 0724356772021)
Release date: 1985
Disc 1: Symphony no. 1 in E Major, op. 26
Westminster Symphonic Choir
Philadelphia Orchestra
Riccardo Muti, conductor
Stefania Toczyska, mezzo-soprano; Michael Myers, tenor

Scriabin, Alexander: *Symphonies*

CD (3 discs): Brilliant Classics (BLC 92744)
Release date: 2006

Disc 1: Symphony no. 1 in E Major, op. 26
See information under original release listing: EMI Classics, 1985

Shostakovich, Dimitri: *Symphony no. 13, op. 113, Babi Yar*

CD: Teldec (TLD 90848)
Release date: 1993
New York Choral Artists
New York Philharmonic
Kurt Masur, conductor
Sergei Leiferkus, bass

Stravinsky, Igor: *Igor Stravinsky: The Composer, Vol. 1*

CD (2 discs): MusicMasters (MM 5375964)
Release date: 1991
Disc 1, Tracks 6–16: *Oedipus Rex*, opera-oratorio in three acts
    New York Choral Artists
    Orchestra of St. Luke's
    Robert Craft, conductor
    Wendy White, Jocasta; Jon Garrison, Oedipus; John Ostendorf,
        Creon; Jon Humphrey, Shepherd; John Cheek, Messenger
Disc 2, Tracks 18–26: *Requiem Canticles*
    New York Choral Artists
    Orchestra of St. Luke's
    Robert Craft, conductor
    Wendy White, mezzo-soprano; John Cheek, bass-baritone
Disc 2, Track 27–29: *Symphony of Psalms*
    New York Choral Artists
    Orchestra of St. Luke's
    Robert Craft, conductor

Wagner, Richard: *Das Liebesmahl der Apostel*

LP: Columbia (LP)
Release date: 1975
Westminster Symphonic Choir
New York Philharmonic
Pierre Boulez, conductor
Yvonne Minton, mezzo-soprano

Wagner, Richard: *Das Liebesmahl der Apostel*

CD: Sony Classical (SMK 68330)
Release date: 1995
See information under original release listing: Columbia, 1975 (remastered for CD in 1995)

Wagner, Richard: *Tannhäuser: Overture & Venusberg Music*

CD: Sony Classical (SK45749)
Release date: 1985
Westminster Symphonic Choir
New York Philharmonic
Zubin Mehta, conductor
The following compilations are in chronological order.

The Westminster Choir Sings Folk Songs

LP: Gothic Records (G 38130)
Release date: 1981
Tracks:
1. Flummerfelt, Joseph (arr.): "Londonderry Air (Danny Boy)"
2. Churchill, Stuart: "Black Is the Color of My True Love's Hair"
3. Parker, Alice and Robert Shaw (arr.): "Annie Laurie"
4. Flummerfelt, Joseph (arr.): "O Waly, Waly"; folk song
5. Vaughan Williams, Ralph: "Turtle Dove"—Robert Phillips, solo
6. Vaughan Williams, Ralph: "Alister McAlpine's Lament"
7. Vaughan Williams, Ralph: "Ca' the Yowes"
8. Kubik, Gail: "O dear! What Can the Matter Be? "
9. Kubik, Gail: "Polly Wolly Doodle"
10. Parker, Alice and Robert Shaw (arr. after Stephen Foster): "Old Folks at Home"
11. Kubik, Gail (arr. after Stephen Foster): "Beautiful Dreamer"
12. Flummerfelt, Joseph (arr.): "Comin' Thro' the Rye"
13. Flummerfelt, Joseph (arr.): "Loch Lomond"
14. Flummerfelt, Joseph (arr.): "Flow Gently, Sweet Afton"

15. Wagner, Roger: "Shenandoah"—Joseph Stephenson, solo
16. Burleigh, Henry T.: "My Lord, What a Morning"
17. Martin, Warren (arr.): "Great Day!"—Joseph Stephenson, solo

Westminster Choir
Joseph Flummerfelt, conductor

Kathleen Battle: *A Christmas Celebration*

CD: EMI Classics (EMI 47587)
Release date: 1986
Tracks:
1. Wade, John Francis: "Adeste fideles, O Come, All Ye Faithful"
2. Adam, Adolphe-Charles: "Minuit, Chrétiens, O Holy Night"
3. Schubert, Franz: *Ellens Gesang III*, D 839/op. 52, no. 6, "Ave Maria"
4. Gruber, Franz Xaver: "Silent Night"
5. Mendelssohn, Felix: "Hark! The Herald Angels Sing"
6. "Un flambeau, Jeannette, Isabelle"
7. "Fum, Fum, Fum"
8. Yon, Pietro: "Gesu Bambino"
9. "I Saw Three Ships"
10. "The First Nowell"
11. "The Holly and the Ivy"
12. Kirkpatrick, William J.: "Away in a Manger"
13. Reger Max: *Schlichte Weisen*, op. 76, no. 52: "Maria Wiegenlied"
14. "Zither Carol"
15. Niles, John Jacob: "I Wonder As I Wander"
16. "Mary Had a Baby"
17. "Rise Up, Shepherd, and Follow"
18. "What Child Is This?"
19. Gounod, Charles (after J. S. Bach): "Ave Maria"
20. "O Come, O Come Emmanuel"
21. Willis, Richard Storrs: "It Came Upon a Midnight Clear"
22. Redner, Lewis H.: "O Little Town of Bethlehem"
23. Praetorious, Michael: "Es ist ein' Ros' entsprungen," from *Musae Sioniae*

New York Choral Artists
Harlem Boys Choir
Orchestra of St. Luke's
Leonard Slatkin, conductor
Kathleen Battle, soprano
George Mims, organ; Robert Wolinsky, harpsichord; Barbara Allen
and Nancy Allen, harp
Music arranged by Michael Gibson, William David Brohn, Robert
Sadin, Nancy Allen, and William Levi Dawson

Horizons—A Musical Journey

CD: Delos Records (DEL 3511)
Release date: 1989
Tracks:
8. Palestrina: "Sicut Cervus"
9. Dvořák: *Stabat Mater*, op. 58/B. 71: "Tui Nati vulnerati"—
   excerpt(s)
See information under original release listings: *Dvořák: Stabat Mater*,
   Delos, 1994 and *Like As a Hart: Psalms & Spiritual Songs*, Chesky,
   1995

O Magnum Mysterium

CD: Chesky Records (CSK 83)
Release date: 1992
Tracks:
1. Foss, Lukas: "Behold, I Build an House"
2. Duruflé, Maurice: *Requiem*, op. 9: "Kyrie"
3. Byrd, William: *Gradualia*, vol. 1, part 2: "Ave verum corpus"
4. Poulenc, Francis: from *Motets (4) pour le temps de Noël*, no. 1,
   "O Magnum Mysterium"
5. Parry, Charles Hubert: "I Was Glad"
6. Britten, Benjamin: *Festival Te Deum* in E Major, op. 32
7. de Victoria, Tomás Luis: "O Magnum Mysterium"
8. Maxwell Davies, Peter: "O Magnum Mysterium"
9. Bainton, Edgar: "And I Saw a New Heaven"
10. Messiaen, Olivier: "O sacrum convivium!"
11. Mozart, Wolfgang Amadeus: "Ave verum corpus," K. 618

12. Verdi, Giuseppe: *Quattro pezzi sacri*, no. 1, "Ave Maria"
13. Bruckner, Anton: "Ave Maria," WAB 6
14. Stravinsky, Igor: "Ave Maria"
15. Brahms, Johannes: "Geistliches Lied," op. 30
16. Lutkin, Peter Christian: "The Lord Bless You and Keep You"

Westminster Choir
Joseph Flummerfelt, conductor
Nancianne Parrella, organ

Compilation: The Kiri Selection

CD: EMI Classics (EMI 545302)
Release date: 1992
Track 4: *Porgy and Bess*: "Summertime"
See information under original release listing: *Kiri Sings Gershwin*, Angel/EMI, 1987

Christmas with the Westminster Choir

CD: Gothic Records (G 49047)
Release date: 1993
Tracks:
1. Wade, John Francis: "O Come All Ye Faithful"
2. "The First Nowell"
3. "O Come, O Come, Emmanuel (Veni Emmanuel)"
4. "Of the Father's Love Begotten (Divinum Mysterium)"
5. Britten, Benjamin: "A Boy Was Born," op. 3
6. Mendelssohn, Felix: "Hark! The Herald Angels Sing"
7. "I Wonder As I Wander"
8. "Angels We Have Heard on High (Gloria)"
9. Hopkins, John Henry: "We Three Kings"
10. "Away in a Manger"
11. Gruber, Franz Xaver: "Silent Night"
12. "Deck the Halls"
13. Handel, George Frideric: "Joy to the World"
14. "Break Forth, O Beauteous"
15. "Sleepers, Awake"
16. "Lo, How a Rose (Es ist ein' Ros')"
17. Leontovych, Mykola: "Carol of the Bells"

18. "O Come Little Children (Ihr Kinderlein kommet)"
19. "From Heaven Above"
20. "Bring a Torch, Jeannette, Isabella (Un Flambeau Jeanette, Isabelle)"
21. "Coventry Carol (Lullay, Lulla, Thou Little Tiny Child)"
22. "While by My Sheep"
23. "What Is this Lovely Fragrance?"
24. "Masters in this Hall"
25. "The Holly and the Ivy"
26. "Go Tell It on the Mountain"
27. "The Twelve Days of Christmas"

Westminster Choir
Joseph Flummerfelt, conductor
Daniel Beckwith, organ

O Come All Ye Faithful

CD: EMI Classics (EMI 315402)
Release date: 1993
Tracks:
1. Wade, John Francis (David Willcocks, arr.): "Adeste fideles"
2. Holst, Gustav (arr.): "Masters in This Hall"
3. "Puer nobis"
4. Flummerfelt, Joseph (arr.): "What Is This Lovely Fragrance?"
5. "In dulci jubilo"
6. Parker, Alice and Robert Shaw (arr.): "O Come, O Come, Emmanuel"
7. Willcocks, David (arr.): "God Rest Ye Merry, Gentlemen"
8. Willcocks, David (arr.): "The First Nowell"
9. Daquin, Louis-Claude: *Nouveau livre de noëls*, op. 2, no. 6, "Noël sur les jeux d'anches, Adam fut un pauvre homme" (organ solo)
10. "Coventry Carol (Lully, Lulla, Thow Littel Tyne Child)"
11. Flummerfelt, Joseph (arr.): "The Holly and the Ivy"
12. Mendelssohn, Felix: "Hark! The Herald Angels Sing"
13. Praetorious, Michael: "Es ist ein' Ros' entsprungen," from *Musae Sioniae*
14. Lojeski, Ed (arr.): "Fum, Fum, Fum"

15. Flummerfelt, Joseph (arr.): "Joseph, lieber Joseph mein"
16. Gruber, Franz Xaver: "Silent Night"
17. Handel, George Friderich (arr. Lowell Mason): "Joy to the World"
18. Daquin, Louis-Claude: *Nouveau livre de noëls*, op. 2, no. 10, "Noël grand-jeu et duo, Quand Dieu naquit à Noël" (organ solo)
19. Nicolai, Philipp: "How Brightly Beams the Morning Star"
20. Jacques, Reginald (arr.): "Good King Wenceslas"
21. Flummerfelt, Joseph (arr.): "Un flambeau, Jeannette, Isabelle"
22. Rutter, John (arr.): "The Twelve Days of Christmas"
23. Leontovych, Mykola (arr. Peter Wilhousky): "Carol of the Bells"
24. Warrel, Arthur (arr.): "A Merry Christmas"

New York Choral Artists
Joseph Flummerfelt, conductor
Douglas Major, organ; Mark Gould and James Pandolfi, trumpets; Julie Landsman, French horn; Joseph Alessi, trombone

Favorite Hymns and Anthems

CD: Gothic Records (G 49044)
Release date: 1994
Tracks:

1. Stanford, Charles Villiers: "When in Our Music God Is Glorified (Engleberg)"
2. Vaughan Williams, Ralph: "O How Amiable"
3. Mendelssohn, Felix: "How Lovely Are the Messengers," from *Paulus*, op. 36
4. "Ye Watchers And Ye Holy Ones (Lasst uns erfreuen)"
5. Arnatt, Ronald: "Lord, Thou Hast Been Our Dwelling-Place"
6. "Guide Me, O Thou Great Jehovah (Tamworth)"
7. Thomson, Virgil: "My Shepherd Will Supply My Need"
8. "For All the Saints (Sine Nomine)"
9. Howells, Herbert: "Like As the Hart Desireth the Water-brooks (Psalm 42)"
10. "Let All the World in Every Corner Sing (High Road)"

11. Vaughan Williams, Ralph: "The King of Love My Shepherd Is (St. Columba)"
12. "How Firm a Foundation (Protection)"
13. York, David Stanley: "Lord Make Me an Instrument"
14. Thompson, Randall: "The Last Words of David"
15. Messiter, Arthur Henry: "Rejoice, Ye Pure in Heart!"
16. "Holy, Holy, Holy (Nicaea)"
17. "Be Thou My Vision (Slane)"
18. "Praise, My Soul, the King of Heaven (Lauda Anima)"
19. "All Praise to Thee, My God, This Night (Tallis' Canon)"
20. Vaughan Williams, Ralph (arr.): "The Hundredth Psalm: All People That on Earth Do Dwell"

Westminster Choir
Joseph Flummerfelt, conductor
Joan Lippincott and Ronald Arnatt, organists

The Only Classical CD (Tape) You'll Ever Need!

CD: RCA Records (RCA 62665)
Release date: 1994
Track 7: Beethoven: Symphony no. 9 "Choral" (excerpts)
See information under original release listing: RCA Records, 1983

Like As a Hart: Psalms & Spiritual Songs

CD: Chesky Records (CSK 138)
Release date: 1995
1. Palestrina, Giovanni: "Sicut cervus"
2. Mendelssohn, Felix: Psalm 42, op. 42: "Wie der Hirsch schreit"
3. Goudimel, Claude: "Ainsi qu'on oil le cerf bruire"
4. Howells, Herbert: *Four Anthems for Chorus*, no. 3: "Like As the Hart Desireth"
5. Boulanger, Lili: Psalm 24, "La terre appartient à l'Éternel"
6. Mozart, Wolfgang Amadeus: "Laudate Dominum"
7. Bruckner, Anton: "Os justi meditabitur sapientiam," WAB 30
8. Ives, Charles: Psalm 67, "God Be Merciful unto Us"
9. Vaughan Williams, Ralph: "O Taste and See"
10. Thomson, Virgil: "My Shepherd Will Supply My Need"

11. Duruflé, Maurice: Notre Père, op. 14
12. Verdi, Giuseppe: "Pater noster"
13. Stravinsky, Igor: "Pater noster"
14. Britten, Benjamin: *Te Deum* in C Major
15. Friedell, Harold: "Draw Us in the Spirit's Tether"
16. Mendelssohn, Felix: "Blessed Are the Men Who Fear Him"
17. Vaughan Williams, Ralph: *Five Mystical Songs*, no. 5: "Antiphon"

Westminster Choir
Joseph Flummerfelt, conductor
Nancianne Parrella, organ

Surround Spectacular—The Music, The Tests

CD (2 discs): Delos Records (DEL 3179)
Release date: 1995
Track 17: Dvořák—*Stabat Mater*, op. 58/B. 71: "Tui Nati vulnerati"
See information under original release listing: *Dvořák: Stabat Mater*, Delos, 1994

The Best Classical Album in the World . . . Ever!

CD: Virgin Classics (PID 678909)
Release date: 1995
Track 26: *Porgy and Bess*: "Summertime"
See information under original release listing: *Kiri Sings Gershwin*, Angel/EMI, 1987

The Classical Collection—Vivaldi, Mozart, Ravel, etc.

CD: Chesky Records (CSK 135)
Release date: 1995
Tracks:
    4. Mozart: *Ave verum corpus* in D Major, K. 618
    9. Foss: "Behold, I Build an House"
See information under original release listing: *O Magnum Mysterium*, Chesky, 1992

Westminster Choir at Spoleto Festival U.S.A.

CD: Gothic Records (G 49078)
Release date: 1996
Tracks:

1. Brahms, Johannes: "O schöne Nacht," op. 92, no. 1
2. Brahms, Johannes: "Warum?," op. 92, no. 4
3. Brahms, Johannes: "Der Gang zum Liebchen," op. 31, no. 3
4. Fauré, Gabriel: "Cantique de Jean Racine," op. 11
5. Hindemith, Paul: *Six Chansons*
6. Morley, Thomas: "Sing We and Chant It"
7. Pilkington, Francis: "Rest, Sweet Nymph"
8. Bartók, Béla: *Four Slovak Songs*
9. Ligeti, György: "Éjszaka (Night)"
10. Flummerfelt, Joseph (arr.): "Loch Lomond"
11. Flummerfelt, Joseph (arr.): "Comin' Thro' the Rye"
12. Copland, Aaron: "The Promise of Living"
13. Shaw/Parker (arr.): "Garden Hymn"
14. Elkins, C., Shaw/Parker (arr.): "His Voice As the Sound"
15. "I Will Arise"
16. Burleigh, H.T. (arr.): "My Lord, What a Mornin'"
17. Shaw, Robert (arr.): "Set Down Servant"
18. Ives, Charles: "Circus Band"
19. Wilhousky, Peter (arr.): "Battle Hymn"
20. Flummerfelt, Joseph (arr.): "Danny Boy"

Westminster Choir
Joseph Flummerfelt, conductor
Glenn Parker and Nancianne Parrella, piano
Rodney Briscoe, bass (track 13)
Heidi Lynn, mezzo-soprano; Levi Hernandez, bass; Alexander Varghese, bass (track 17)

Engineer's Choice 2

CD: Delos Records (DEL 3512)
Release date: 1997
Track 10: Mussorgsky: *Sorochintsy Fair*: "The Peasant Lad's Dream Vision"

See information under original release listings: *Heaven and Hell*, Delos, 1997

Serene Journeys Through Classical Music

CD (3 discs): Delos Records (DEL 1608)
Release date: 1998
Track 37: Dvořák—*Stabat Mater*, op. 58/B. 71: "Tui Nati vulnerati"
See information under original release listing: *Dvořák: Stabat Mater*, Delos, 1994

Kiri: Handel, Mozart, Puccini, et al.

CD: EMI Classics (EMI 572312)
Release date: 2001
Track 14: *Porgy and Bess*: "Summertime"
See information under original release listing: *Kiri Sings Gershwin*, Angel/EMI, 1987

Kurt Masur at the New York Philharmonic, Vol. 1

CD (3 discs): The Philharmonic-Symphony Society of New York, Inc. (NYP 0104)
Release date: 2001
New York Philharmonic
Kurt Masur, conductor
Discs 1–2: J. S. Bach: *The Passion According to St. Matthew* (BWV 244) (1993)
    Westminster Symphonic Choir
    Edith Wiens, soprano; Carolyn Watkinson, mezzo-soprano; Peter Schreier, tenor; Andreas Schmidt, baritone; Alastair Miles, bass
Disc 3: Claude Debussy: *Le Martyre de St. Sébastien* (1997)
    Westminster Symphonic Choir
    Maria Ewing, narrator; Elizabeth Norberg-Schulz, soprano; Nancy Maultsby, mezzo-soprano; Mary Ann McCormick, mezzo-soprano

Kurt Masur at the New York Philharmonic, Vol. 2

CD (2 discs): The Philharmonic-Symphony Society of New York, Inc. (NYP 0105)

Release date: 2001
Disc 1: Ludwig van Beethoven: *Missa solemnis* in D Major, op. 123 (1999)
New York Choral Artists
Sylvia McNair, soprano; Florence Quivar, mezzo-soprano; Stuart Neill, tenor; René Pape, bass
Disc 2: Ludwig van Beethoven: Symphony no. 9 in D minor, op. 125, *Choral* (1999)
The New Years Eve Concert of the Millennium
New York Choral Artists
Christine Brewer, soprano; Florence Quivar, mezzo-soprano; Anthony Rolfe Johnson, tenor; Peter Rose, bass

Kurt Masur at the New York Philharmonic, Vol. 5

CD (3 discs): The Philharmonic-Symphony Society of New York, Inc. (NYP 0108)
Release date: 2001
Disc 2: Igor Stravinsky: *Perséphone, a Melodrama in Three Tableaux* (1999)
Marthe Keller, narrator
Stuart Neill, tenor
Disc 3: Arthur Honegger: *Jeanne d'Arc au Bûcher* (1994)
Marthe Keller, Jeanne; David Wilson-Johnson, Frère Dominique; Heidi Grant Murphy, soprano; D'Anna Fortunato, soprano; Wendy Hoffman, contralto; John Aler, tenor; Nathaniel Watson, bass

The Opera Album

CD (2 discs): EMI Classics (EMI 678302)
Release date: 2002
Track 35: *Porgy and Bess*: "Summertime"
See information under original release listing: *Kiri Sings Gershwin*, Angel/EMI, 1987

Classical Legends

CD: EMI Classics (EMI 625012B)
Release date: 2003
Track 17: *Porgy and Bess*: "Summertime"

See information under original release listing: *Kiri Sings Gershwin*, Angel/EMI, 1987

The Very Best of Jessye Norman

CD (2 discs): EMI Classics (EMI 759122)
Release date: 2003
Disc 2, Track 5: Berlioz, *Roméo et Juliette*, op. 17: "Premiere transports—Strophes"
See information under original release listing: *Berlioz—Roméo et Juliette*, EMI Classics, 1986

The Very Best of Kiri Te Kanawa

CD: EMI Classics (EMI 851112)
Release date: 2003
Tracks:
    17. *George White's Scandals of 1924*: "Somebody Loves Me"
    18. *The Goldwyn Follies*: "Love Is Here To Stay"
    19. *Girl Crazy*: "Embraceable You"
    20. *Porgy and Bess*: "Summertime"
See information under original release listing: *Kiri Sings Gershwin*, Angel/EMI, 1987

Euphoric Classics: A Classical High—Strauss, Bach, et al.

CD (2 discs): EMI Classics (EMI 625112)
Release date: 2004
Disc 1, Track 5: Symphony no. 9 "Choral": "Ode to Joy"
See information under original release listing: Angel/EMI, 1999

Heaven To Earth

CD: Avie Records (AVIE 0046)
Release date: 2004
Tracks:
    1. Barber, Samuel: *Agnus Dei*, op. 11
    2. Duruflé, Maurice: *Requiem*, op. 9: "Introit"
    3. Duruflé, Maurice: *Requiem*, op. 9: "Kyrie"
    4. Ives, Charles: Psalm 90, "Lord, Thou Hast Been"

5. Bernstein, Leonard: *Chichester Psalms*, no. 2: "Adonai ro-i lo ehsar"
6. Stravinsky, Igor: "Credo"
7. Stravinsky, Igor: "Pater noster"
8. Vaughan Williams, Ralph: *Five Mystical Songs*, no. 3: "Love Bade Me Welcome"
9. Vaughan Williams, Ralph: *Five Mystical Songs*, no. 4: "The Call"
10. Verdi, Giuseppe: *Quattro pezzi sacri*, no. 1: "Ave Maria"
11. Schoenberg, Arnold: "Friede auf Erden," op. 13

Westminister Choir
Joseph Flummerfelt, conductor
Nancianne Parrella, organ
Francois Suhr, boy soprano (track 5)
Charles Robert Stephens, baritone (tracks 8, 9)
Recorded at Princeton University Chapel

Best Classics 100 Vol. 2

CD: EMI Classics (EMI 708722)
Release date: 2006
Track 4: *Porgy and Bess*: "Summertime"
See information under original release listing: *Kiri Sings Gershwin*, Angel/EMI, 1987

INDEX

185

ABOUT THE SUBJECT AND AUTHOR

Musical America's 2004 Conductor of the Year, **Joseph Flummerfelt** is among the most accomplished and sought-after choral conductors in the world. He has collaborated with the world's greatest orchestras and conductors and his work may be heard in over forty recordings

Flummerfelt was raised in Vincennes, Indiana; his mother taught piano and his father was a funeral director. He attended DePauw University in Greencastle, Indiana, studying organ and church music. Upon graduating, he studied with Roger Wagner and Julius Herford in San Diego. He received his master of music degree from the Philadelphia Conservatory of Music, working there and at Singing City Choir with Elaine Brown, then continued his studies with Nadia Boulanger at Fontainebleau in France. Flummerfelt returned to DePauw University as head of choral activities (1964–1968), then held the same title at Florida State University in Tallahassee (1968–1971). In 1971, he completed his doctoral degree at the University of Illinois where he studied with Harold Decker, began as *Maestro del coro* at Il Festival dei Due Mondi in Spoleto, Italy (the first year with the Florida State Choir and subsequent years with the Westminster Choir), and began a thirty-three year tenure at Westminster Choir College, where he was artistic director. That same year he also began as principal choral director at the New York Philharmonic, a position he continues to hold.

During his time of artistic leadership as Westminster Choir College, his choirs sang most of the great works of the Western canon in New York City and Philadelphia with the greatest orchestras of the world, including the New York Philharmonic, the Philadelphia Orchestra, the Berlin Philharmonic, the Vienna Philharmonic, the Leipzig Gewandhaus, the New Jersey Symphony Orchestra, and the San Francisco Symphony. Flummerfelt was part of the team around Gian Carlo Menotti who formed Spoleto

USA in Charleston, South Carolina in 1977; he remains artistic director of choral activities there. He returned to Singing City Choir as artistic director from 1994 to 1999.

Flummerfelt has won many awards and honors, including the Prix de President de la Republique, L'Academie de Disque Français (1973, for Messiaen's *Transfiguration of Our Lord Jesus Christ*), Mobil Oil Pegasus Award (1975, for his contribution to the Spoleto Festival in Italy), and honorary doctoral degrees from Purdue University, Vincennes University, Ursinus College, and DePauw University. He has won numerous Grammy awards, including that for the acclaimed recording of John Adams' *On the Transmigration of Souls* with Lorin Maazel and the New York Philharmonic. His recording of the works of Johannes Brahms with the Westminster Choir, *Singing for Pleasure*, was chosen by the *New York Times* as a favorite among all existing Brahms recordings.

Flummerfelt has had numerous works composed for his choirs, most notably Carlisle Floyd's *A Time to Dance* for the Westminster Choir and the San Antonio Symphony, and Stephen Paulus's *Voices of Light* for the Westminster Choir and the New York Philharmonic. He has guest-conducted the New York Philharmonic, Orchestra of St. Luke's, Honolulu Symphony, San Antonio Symphony, Phoenix Symphony, Spoleto Festival Orchestra (USA and Italy), Bochumer Symphoniker (Germany), and the Juilliard Symphony Orchestra. He is a revered teacher of conducting and travels widely for workshops and guest conducting.

Donald Nally was raised in Hilltown, Pennsylvania, a rural community in Upper Bucks County. He first attended Mansfield State College (now University), then received his undergraduate degree at the University of Cincinnati's College-Conservatory of Music, after which he chaired the music department at Chicago's Performing Arts High School. In 1985 he began studies with Joseph Flummerfelt at Westminster Choir College in Princeton, New Jersey, earning a master's degree in choral conducting. Doctoral studies followed at the University of Illinois under Don V. Moses; Nally completed the degree with a dissertation on the relationship of words to music in the choral works of Samuel Barber.

Throughout his graduate studies, Nally became increasingly involved with the Spoleto Festivals in Italy and Charleston, having first sung there as a member of the Westminster Choir under Flummerfelt. In 1994, the festivals split and he succeeded Flummerfelt as director of choirs at Il Festival dei

Due Mondi, working closely with Gian Carlo Menotti on programming, as well as conducting concerts and operas at the festival. During this time he was chorus master at the Opera Company of Philadelphia (1992–2003) and assistant professor of music at West Chester University (1992–1996). He founded the short-lived professional choir, the Bridge Ensemble, in 1996, then served as artistic director of the Choral Arts Society of Philadelphia (1998–2002) and director of music at St. Mark's Church, Philadelphia (1997–2003). Under his direction, the Choral Arts Society won the 2002 Chorus America Margaret Hillis National Award for Excellence in Choral Music.

In 2003 Nally became chorus master at Welsh National Opera, moving to the United Kingdom where he also regularly worked with the Philharmonia Chorus of London. In 2005, he joined with a group of friends in Philadelphia to form the professional choir, The Crossing. Dedicated to new music, the ensemble won the 2009 ASCAP/Chorus America Award for Adventuresome Programming. Nally moved to Chicago in 2007 to begin work as chorus master at Lyric Opera of Chicago. He continues to conduct The Crossing in Philadelphia as well as Cincinnati's Vocal Arts Ensemble, where he is music director.

Known for his refined performances of new music, he has been called "the choral czar of Philadelphia" in the press. He has worked with many of the great artistic minds of today's concert halls and opera houses.